Between Life and Eternity

A true story about a terrible wreck,

an encounter with an angel,

and future events

Bob Bell

Between Life and Eternity

Published by:
Intermedia Publishing, Inc.
P.O. Box 2825
Peoria, Arizona 85380
www.intermediapub.com

ISBN 978-1-937654-50-4
Copyright © 2012 by Capt. Bob Bell
and Encounter Publishing, L.L.C.
www.encounterpublishingllc.com
Printed in the United States of America

Scripture quotations have been taken from the King James Version of the Holy Bible unless indicated otherwise.
Scripture taken from the HOLY BIBLE, NEW INTERNATIONAL VERSION®. Copyright © 1973, 1978, 1984 Biblica. Used by permission of Zondervan. All rights reserved.

CONTENTS

DEDICATION

To God who hears our cries, sends His angel, and saves us.

FOREWORD

My friend Bob Bell has spent thirty years of his life as a Navy JAG officer/attorney handling cases for the United States Navy. He also worked as a civilian trial lawyer representing numerous high profile insurance companies, including Lloyd's of London. Professional and highly educated, Bob graduated from Emory Law School, one of the top schools in the country. I know him personally and also know he has absolutely no motive to concoct, embellish, or even reveal the details of his story. In fact, Bob would rather *not* tell his story at all because he's aware many people will look at him with raised eyebrows, questioning his veracity. Yet, he feels compelled to share his story because it brings hope and comfort to hurting people. It also shows us God is real, knows each of us intimately, and that He is working in our lives even though we often cannot see or understand our circumstances. In addition, Bob's story reveals that God is actively involved in the affairs of nations, particularly the United States. God is not just sitting on the sidelines to predict or referee human events. God often brings about His plans on Earth by using regular people like you and me.

The supernatural events chronicled in the following pages are true, and I'm excited for you to read them. As you do, you will find hope replacing despair and faith replacing fear. I know I did.

Max Davis, Bestselling author of seventeen books including the upcoming ING series with painter Ron DiCianni.

PART I

THE WRECK AND AFTERMATH

PROLOGUE
A MOTHER'S LOVE

July 20, 1984, in the middle of the night, my mother Roselle received a telephone call all mothers dread the most, telling her that her son Bob and his family were involved in a serious wreck. Bob was in critical condition in the Intensive Care Unit at North Miami General Hospital. With no more specific information, she was advised to come to the hospital as quickly as possible. In her Cairo, Georgia home north of Tallahassee, she quickly prepared for her emergency journey and drove to the Tallahassee Airport in the pre-dawn hours to board the earliest flight to Miami.

Upon arriving, she took a taxi directly to the hospital and was immediately directed to the ICU, but she was in severe shock and greatly distressed when she entered the ICU. She could not find Bob. He looked so horrible from his injuries and was bandaged so much she could not recognize her own son among the ICU patients. She began desperately crying and calling his name over and over again. Bob roused enough from his dazed stupor to blurt out, "Mom, it's me." She instantly recognized his voice and knew which patient was Bob. She was still very upset but tried to talk quietly to comfort him.

CHAPTER 1
FLASHPOINT

"Oh, God, he's going to hit us," Muffin cried as an oncoming truck veered directly into our path. In the next instant, I heard a thunderous shout above us, followed almost simultaneously by a magnificent burst of light with a single beam shooting down towards Earth, both illuminating and enveloping everything around us. Racing down the beam of light with amazing speed was what appeared to be an ancient soldier, armed with a sword and wearing a military kilt that came down just below his knees. I was galvanized by this shocking, spectacular sight. Then, just as quickly as he appeared, he was gone. As hard as it was to comprehend, the entire electrifying episode happened in a split second while time seemed to be moving in slow-motion.

Snapping back to the grim reality of the speeding truck hurling towards us, I instinctively jerked our car slightly to the right so my side of the car would bear the brunt of the brutal crash that was coming. I wasn't trying to be a hero. I was terrified, but I hoped my desperate, split-second maneuver would spare the lives of my wife, Muffin and of our two and a half-year-old daughter, Elizabeth. I bravely braced for impact.

As the truck smashed into my side of the car, I momentarily saw the eyes of the other driver, glowing strangely red and evil. The truck rode up over the hood of our Toyota, its front tires crushing our windshield and obliterating our dashboard. Glass shards flew everywhere, embedding in my face and head. The force of the impact broke the metal frames of my eyeglasses, but the shatterproof lenses protected my eyes for an instant before the lenses dropped to the floor. Then, a strange thing happened. The man in the ancient battle dress suddenly appeared again, coming between me and the truck, pushing it away from me with a super-human strength. I was absolutely amazed and awed and also gripped with instant gratitude that he was coming to the rescue. No mere man could do what he had just done. Then, he disappeared again.

Stunned and dazed, I leaned over to check on Muffin. Even though she was unresponsive, I kissed her cheek and told her I loved her. I then told her goodbye in case one or both of us did not survive. I heard some sounds from Elizabeth, but I could not see into the other side of the back seat where she was in her car safety seat. It was dark, I did not have my glasses, and the roof of the car was collapsed on that side.

Suddenly, I was aware of someone talking to me through my open window. It was the driver of the truck, seemingly unharmed. He leaned in close to my face in the dark and asked loudly, "Is anyone alive in there?"

"Yes," I cried. "We need help."

"Don't worry," he yelled back, "you won't live long." With that, he ran away from the scene, leaving us to die.

In one frantic attempt, I struggled to get out of the car to go help Muffin and Elizabeth on the other side. Somehow, I managed to get out of the car. The effort caused me to collapse on the pavement close to the oncoming line of vehicles. As the headlights went by me in seemingly endless succession, I lay on my back in the road, drifting in and out of consciousness, yet with a dazed, general awareness of my surroundings. I was cold and shivering. Someone came and put something over me as I lay there to try to keep me warm and stop the shivering that was shaking me as I was losing consciousness. Then the curtain of death came down over my life, and I lost consciousness completely.

Immediately after I finally lost all consciousness at the scene of the wreck, I somehow saw my precious wife as her spirit separated from her physical body. Her new body glowed with radiant energy. Then, I saw Elizabeth. She, too, had separated from her physical body and was playing around her mother. I realized at that moment, I, too, had separated from my physical body and was free of pain.

As we separated from our bodies, the ancient warrior appeared again, coming to the rescue. This time, though, he was glowing with an even brighter aura of energy about him. I realized, finally, he must be an angel, although I did not know his name. For the first time, I noticed his military garb was colored in shades of white, including very light gold and beige, although the shades and colors were somewhat obscured by the glow of light surrounding him. The beam of light that appeared from the sky just before the impact was now like a stairway or escalator. That's the best way I can describe it. The angel started ascending the stairway toward Heaven. Muffin turned to follow him. When Elizabeth did not follow, Muffin turned around, looked at me and Elizabeth and called her to come. Elizabeth lingered just a moment longer, still frolicking about, but she soon followed her mother as instructed.

I, too, started to follow both of them up the moving stairway so we could stay together, but the angel saw what I was doing and came back to me. "Stop," he shouted, "your time has not come yet. You still have work to be done on earth." He stuck his hand in my chest and forcefully, but not violently, shoved me back down the stairway of light. It was then I saw Muffin kneel and bow in humble adoration when she reached the top of the stairway. She and Elizabeth soon disappeared out of sight as if going over a hill. There was a glow of light coming from the other side, along with sounds of music, celebration, and joy.

I was tremendously grateful they were in Heaven, but I was emotionally shattered that I was not going there with them. "Why can't I die and be with my wife and daughter?" I frantically pleaded with the angel.

"If you choose to die when you can live," he counseled, "that would be a sin and could be held against you. It may not be advisable for you to choose to die when you can live, as you may face judgment in that condition." The angel also told me if I died, the man who killed my wife and daughter would get away with his crime. He told me this man had previously gotten away with many evil things and that God was ready to bring him to justice. I needed to live and be an eyewitness to his crime. If I lived, other witnesses would be discovered and would come forward to testify against this man.

I definitely did not want the man who killed my wife and daughter to go unpunished, but I certainly did not want to be separated from them either. There was no satisfactory solution to the situation. Earlier, while I was drifting in and out of consciousness lying on my back near my car, I heard the paramedics on the scene say every bone in my body was broken. "I don't want to live as an invalid, I would rather be dead," I argued angrily with the angel, attempting to change his action that was brutally blocking my path to my family.

"You will not have any broken bones," he promised. "You will be healed." He reached out with his sword and touched my left arm at the elbow. I felt a surge of healing energy, fusing my bones together again. While I was immensely grateful for his healing touch, I wondered why he touched my left elbow when my entire right side was badly injured. He told me for the healing energy to be most effective it needed to enter my body through an area that was whole. Apparently, my left elbow was one area of my body that was not injured.

As I wrestled with issues of life and death with the angel, the driver of the truck fled down the embankment of a nearby canal, hiding in the bushes in the water ....

CHAPTER 2
UNEXPECTED HELP

Young Sam Reynolds, Jr., (Name has been changed. As I learned later, young Sam was the teenage son of one of the partners at my previous law firm.) lived in a nearby home with his parents. He decided to walk to the K-Mart Shopping Center before it closed at 10 p.m. He was walking on the sidewalk near the shopping center when he witnessed a terrible accident. He saw the mangled wreckage and knew instantly this was a very bad situation. He saw the driver of the truck get out and look around the wreckage of the other car. That same man leaned in the driver's side window of the wrecked, twisted yellow Toyota lift-back. Then Sam saw the driver of the truck flee. Sam, a teenager, decided to follow him.

Sam kept quiet and tailed the man at a safe distance. He saw the man go down the bank of a canal and hide carefully in the water among some bushes growing along the shoreline. Sam then turned back to the wreckage and saw another man lying badly injured in the road alongside the driver's side of the Toyota. He saw a passerby, a woman who had stopped her car and locked her own young daughter in the car so she could aid the mangled man in the street. The woman grabbed a beach towel with an unusual geometric pattern from her car and placed it atop the man in the road who was in shock, shivering and shaking uncontrollably.

Sam waited anxiously for the police and emergency medical technicians to arrive on the scene. When they arrived, Sam realized just how horrible the accident was. The lady in the Toyota was dead. Her young daughter in the back seat was critically injured. The unconscious, dying man lying motionless on his back on the pavement was near death with multiple broken bones. The EMT's were preparing to transport the young two-year-old to the nearest hospital but not the now lifeless man. The unusual beach towel was pulled up to completely cover the maimed man's body and face. The EMT's were temporarily unconcerned about the man's corpse and focused their attention on trying to help the young child who was still alive.

The policemen on the scene questioned Sam. They asked him what he saw. They wanted to know, "Where is the driver of the truck?" Sam replied, "Follow me." Sam led the officers to the bank of the canal and pointed to a clump of bushes. "That's where he's hiding." The officers pointed their flashlights at the hiding spot and ordered the driver to come out and surrender. The driver of the truck refused. Finally, the police called the Florida Marine Patrol. They sent a boat to enter the canal from Biscayne Bay to arrest the suspect. After his eventual arrest, tests at a local hospital confirmed what everyone feared: a very high level of alcohol and illegal drugs in his body.

The suspect's injuries were minor....

CHAPTER 3
BETWEEN LIFE AND ETERNITY

While my body lay badly broken and lifeless on the pavement, I continued to experience an argument with the angel, a confrontation outside the normal dimensions of time and space, or what is referred to as an out-of-body, near-death episode. Even though I knew the angel had infused my body with healing energy, I wanted to support my arguments against him by using what I heard earlier when the paramedics were discussing my broken bones. So I assertively asked the angel, "If it takes time for me to recover from my injuries and learn to walk again, how will I support myself financially? What will I do for money as I am self-employed, and my law practice is my only source of income?"

The angel patiently explained to me that I had twice the amount of coverage with my automobile insurance policy than I thought I had. The money I received would more than cover my medical and personal living expenses. While I thought the angel was surely mistaken, I was afraid to confidently contradict him. Facing his overpowering display of might and authority, I was overwhelmed. My contentious will was crushed. My fighting spirit was supernaturally subdued in the struggle. The angel assured me God would take care of my needs. He wasn't going to let me use money as a reason to join my wife and daughter in Heaven! My next argument as I verbally wrestled with the angel....

I pleaded pathetically with the angel to let me go to Heaven because I did not want to continue life alone without my family. His response seemed to be cruel and callous. He told me I would certainly not be alone, that I could have another family if I wanted. His answer made me angry. I wanted my family back that I already had! I tried to continue to argue with the angel, but he became more emphatic and specific, showing me more about my future family. This argument was not going to persuade the angel either.

I was stunned by this situation that was way beyond anything I could ever have imagined being involved in, but I continued to press my arguments to the angel with everything I could muster that was apparently relevant. In desperation, I pushed back against the angel's stonewall of negative responses to my painful predicament. As all of my appeals to the angel based on personal reasons were completely rejected, I lunged into my assumed best moral point, lambasting the angel: "But if I live, what will be my purpose in life?" He came closer now, looked into my eyes and began to explain why I had to live. At this point, he was less like a warrior and more like a loving, compassionate Jesus. He truly wanted to help me understand and realize the importance of my life's work.

He said, "If you die, first your clients will lose all their cases because no other lawyer will help them." I thought he was probably right about that, but I did not want to agree with him. I wanted to win the life and death argument with the angel for me and my family, but it was true that nobody else wanted my cases that often involved international travel, foreign languages, and highly specialized areas of maritime law that were more difficult to handle. The angel hit me below the belt with his comment about the content of my cases, but then he softened his next statement somewhat, pointing out that my mission was to help people in general, not just those with legal problems. Now I was stuck with a broader purpose that would be harder to avoid argumentatively.

I had no choice. I must continue to talk persuasively to the angel in a last ditch effort to change the outcome. I wondered out loud how I would know whom to help. He assured me I would know in each situation when I was to help someone. Next, he told me something that was a super shocker.

He asserted I would have a future important role in national defense. I thought the angel had really missed the issue now. I was ready to retire from the Navy Reserve in less than two years, giving me twenty years of service. I could retire as a Navy Commander, which was good enough for me. I had no burning ambition to achieve any higher rank. I already had a distinguished, unblemished Navy career with several major accomplishments along with an abundance of regular duty. I had achieved much more than I thought possible. I looked forward to spending more time with my wife and family. I was definitely planning to retire soon. The angel assured me however, retirement was not in my near future.

The angel must have seen from the expression on my face I was deeply upset and exhausted. I was running out of my ineffective arguments to use against his overpowering authority and the apparently unchanging inevitable tragic outcome. He compassionately stretched out his hand and took my hand. He said, "Come with me. I will show you some things to help you understand." He showed me the Soviet atrocities in Afghanistan at the time: the Red Army using chemical weapons on men, women, and children; the skin and flesh falling off their faces even if they did not die; the maiming for life of so many children. Then he took me to Russia itself and showed me the oppression there, including the concentration camps in Siberia.

I could hear the cries of the people rising up from the communist countries and asked the angel if he heard them, too. "Yes," he said, "and the Lord has also heard their cries for many years just as he heard the cries of His people in Egypt for 400 years. But the Lord is getting ready to act. He will soon bring down the communist regime in Russia."

The angel showed me future mass demonstrations at the time of the downfall of communist rule in Eastern Europe and Russia itself. I had never seen such vast hordes of desperate people assembled together in public gatherings. I saw endless multitudes of them stretching into Red Square and The Kremlin in Moscow itself. I wanted to see and know more, but the angel hurried to leave. He said my exposure to high levels of energy and radiation from this eternal environment outside of time could cause me serious harm. I still had more questions, hoping vainly to bring up something that would help my failing arguments, so I innocently asked, "How am I involved in this? How does this relate to me?"

His answer confused and frightened me more than anything else he told me so far. He pointed his index finger at me and said bluntly, "Your job is to make sure the United States is prepared to fight and win World War III." Now I was even more exasperated as I cried out: "What am I supposed to do?"

I wanted to continue to argue with the angel to try to change the deadly result so I could be with Muffin and Elizabeth, but the angel began fading from my view now when I needed him to help me. He simply said, "When the time comes, you will know what you are supposed to do. You will not be taken by surprise."

And with those final perplexing powerful words, he disappeared, leaving me with my unwanted missions and orders from Higher Authority, as I returned to life with an awareness of my presence at the scene of the wreck.

CHAPTER 4
LEFT TO DIE

As I was regaining consciousness, I heard the EMT's talking, but I could not see them. Something was covering my face. At first, they were not close enough for me to understand what they were saying. Then one of the EMT's spoke louder and more clearly, announcing, "Well, it's time to clean up the scene of the accident and take the bodies to the morgue." When I heard this, I made a maximum effort to move. I tried to sit up, and the beach towel fell off my face. I was unable to raise myself and fell back onto the pavement, but now I could see the EMT's. However, they were blurred and hazy. I did not have my glasses. It was dark. I was trying to regain my focus, and I was enduring overwhelming pain. The other paramedic noticed my movement and checked me over again. Amazed, he shouted out, "We can't take him to the morgue because he ain't dead yet. We will have to take him to the hospital." The first EMT replied dismally, "Well, it won't do any good because he's going to die anyway. Every bone in his body is broken."

After my life was restored, I could not even raise myself up off the pavement. Yet God had raised me from the dead. This was a phenomenal part of the angel's promise that I would be healed. Strange as it may seem, I did not even think about the astounding fact I had been raised from the dead. I did not fully realize I had been physically dead because during the time my body was lifeless, I was alive in another dimension preoccupied with experiencing the encounter with the angel. Then I was suddenly thrust back into life into a severe survival mode, confronting pessimistic personnel who seemed to think I was as good as dead no matter what.

I knew I still had very serious injuries, but I also knew my broken bones had been miraculously healed by the angel. So I made a second effort to sit up to show them I still had life and the will to survive. The paramedic told me to lie down because my movement could make my injuries worse. They put me on a stretcher, loaded me into the ambulance, and took me to the nearest emergency room. The ambulance ride was excruciatingly painful for me. I remember asking them to please slow down as the fast motion and sharp turns caused me unbearable pain. I also asked about my daughter. They told me she was already at the hospital, but they did not know her condition.

I do not remember who gave me some pain medication, but I do remember waking up inside the hospital, lying on my back on a rolling stretcher against a wall in the hallway of the emergency room. I heard a group of doctors conferring about my case a short distance away. One doctor argued, "Nothing can be done for him. He is going to die anyway. Besides, he's a lawyer. If we try to help him, one of his lawyer friends will sue us after he dies, blaming us for his death." With a sense of panic, I realized even though an angel had healed me and told me to go on living, I could be left to die in the hospital. I wondered if God's miracle in my body would be wasted through human neglect. I realized I must do something immediately to change the doctors' minds.

I motioned with my right hand for the lead doctor to come to my side. As he came closer to my face, I whispered, "Doctor, it is true I am a lawyer, but I am a lawyer who represents doctors, nurses, and hospitals. I have never lost one of those cases." The doctor was stunned by my comments. He turned to the other doctors and with great emphasis said, "He is a lawyer, but he is one of our lawyers. We must make an effort to save him."

While all the doctors still argued among themselves, one of them interjected, "Why don't we just take some x-rays? Nobody could ever fault us for just taking x-rays." All the doctors suddenly agreed with this procedure. I was immediately wheeled upstairs to the x-ray room. After the technician took a full set of x-rays, he commented skeptically, "Something must be wrong with the film. It's not showing anything." Then he took a second full set with new film and again exclaimed incredulously, "Something is still wrong. The x-rays show nothing. It must be the x-ray equipment." As he prepared to take yet another full set of x-rays, I motioned for him to come over. I told him, "There is nothing wrong with your film or your equipment. Please just give up and show the film to the doctors. I'm not as badly injured as the EMT's reported."

Soon, I was returned to the emergency room where the doctors really got busy treating me. They realized they were close to letting a patient die who could be saved. They realized they could be charged with gross negligence if they refused to treat me. From this point on, I received the best of care. A plastic surgeon was called in to deal with my facial injuries and the multitude of glass fragments embedded in my forehead and scalp.

After some time in the emergency room, I was asked about next of kin. I did not realize this meant Muffin was dead. Because I had not received any information about my wife or daughter, I feared they really were dead. Hours after the accident, Muffin's parents came in to see me. They told me Muffin and Elizabeth were both dead. I knew then what I experienced in my encounter with the angel was really true. Muffin and Elizabeth were in Heaven together.

Muffin's parents also told me they loved me and would help me. At the same time my cousin John drove to the hospital in the middle of the night with some photographs the plastic surgeon requested. John consented to my treatment and the necessary procedures. Then the plastic surgeon got to work. He removed the larger fragments of glass from my forehead and scalp. The smaller shards were left embedded in my flesh under my skin because trying to remove them with a surgical knife would do more harm than good. Using the family photographs, he straightened and shortened my nose to look like me again. He grafted skin to cover part of my face where skin was missing and chunks of flesh were carved out by flying glass. When he finished, the plastic surgeon planned to follow up with me in several weeks. He had done everything he could to restore my nose and face to look like me again.

I had a serious concussion and other injuries. I kept a small fold-up umbrella on the front seat of the car by my right leg. The force of the impact pushed the metal ribs of the umbrella into my right thigh, mangling it. I was paralyzed from the waist down. I had back and nerve injuries in my lower back and pelvic area.

My mother Roselle was already frantic when she arrived at the hospital from Tallahassee after receiving very limited information about my condition in the middle of the night. She had been told that Muffin and Elizabeth were both dead. After walking into the ICU and recognizing me from my voice, she was in severe shock. She was very upset about my injuries and tearfully grieving the loss of Muffin and her only granddaughter Elizabeth. To console her, I told her about my encounter with the angel, and she stopped crying so much. She believed in God and believed what I told her.

After my mother spent some time with me, she needed to rest and left to stay with Muffin's Aunt Pat and Uncle Bill who lived very close to the hospital. As I lay alone in the ICU struggling with sorrow and enduring intense pain, fitfully drifting off to sleep and just as frequently waking up again, I had a flashback about Muffin and our life together.

CHAPTER 5
WHO'S THAT GIRL

Each of us has cause to think with deep gratitude of those who have lighted the flame within us.

- Albert Schweitzer

While I was angry about Muffin's death and grieving her loss, I remembered fondly how we met in an "it was meant to be" situation. This good memory temporarily replaced in my mind the tragic reality of Muffin's sudden death at such a young age when our wonderful lives together and our family were apparently just getting well established.

New Year's Eve Dance, The Bath Club on Miami Beach, 1972—I didn't have a date, but I attended the dance with friends. The evening provided pleasant company and a retreat from the grind of work. After I moved to Miami from Tallahassee, these social events were a way for me to meet new people. Later in the evening, as I was engaged in lively conversation at one of the tables, I suddenly saw a very attractive, classy-looking girl with straight, shoulder-length brown hair on the dance floor. There was something special about her: the way she carried herself, the aura she projected. I turned to an older lady at my table, the lady who usually knew everything about everyone, a virtual walking social encyclopedia, and whispered, "Who's that girl?" With a disdainful tone and a smug look on her face, she responded with, "Oh, that's the Elliott girl, but she is not available. She is dating that boy she's dancing with, so forget about her!" The lady didn't even tell me the beautiful girl's first name.

Early summer, 1973—Some of the officers of the Bachelors' and Spinsters' Clubs complained the club members were not meeting each other enough, so they decided to host an early evening mixer at a member's home. While the names of these clubs were somewhat old-fashioned, membership in them provided a way for single professionals to meet each other at social events. I was a member of the Bachelors' Club, and while I tired of the usual string of social activities, I decided to attend the evening mixer. As I walked through the front door, I was pleasantly surprised to see the "Elliott girl" standing next to the entrance, talking with her friend, Cathy. While I still did not know the beautiful woman's first name, I did know Cathy and decided to strike up a conversation with her as a way of introduction to the "Elliott girl" who looked stunning in a white lace summer dress. When Cathy's boyfriend came over and asked Cathy to dance, she turned to me and said, "Bob, dance with Muffin, while I dance with Bill." That was the icebreaker I had hoped for! I finally knew her name! Muffin and I talked in earnest for quite a while after that. As she said goodbye some time later, I asked for her number. She said only, "It's Elliott on Banyan Drive." This girl was going to make me work to ask her out! I eventually found her number, and we slowly began a friendship and dating relationship lasting three years while Muffin finished her Master's degree in Psychiatric Social Work at Barry University in Miami. In addition to her beauty and poise, I was thoroughly impressed by Muffin's vigorous, idealistic views. She deeply admired Dr. Albert Schweitzer for his life of humanitarian work in Africa, a life of service she wanted to emulate. Throughout our dating relationship, I accompanied her to many encounter groups that were part of her required studies for her degree. I learned much about the counseling and service that was her life's calling.

As our relationship progressed and the subject of marriage came up, Muffin indicated she wanted to elope. While that sounded like the perfect way to get married without all the hassles of planning a big wedding, I wondered how I could plan a really classy, fun, memorable elopement with our limited resources! Then in July, 1976, I drove to Newport, Rhode Island, so that I could enroll in a special operational course at the Naval War College for my two-week active duty assignment. Faced with the grim reminders of our fragile mortality that were starkly intertwined in the course, I developed a new sense of urgency not to waste life's precious opportunities. The blessings of today could be gone tomorrow. I decided now was the time, and this was the place to elope! I telephoned Muffin and asked if she would like to fly up to Boston to get married! She liked the idea very much. She had attended college in Boston and loved New England. So two weeks later, she and her parents, as well as a special aunt and uncle and a close friend who would serve as her maid of honor, flew to Boston. In the meantime, with the help of my cousin Dr. Peyton Richter who taught philosophy at Boston University, I made arrangements with a pastor he knew at a church in nearby Rockport, Massachusetts. Our rehearsal luncheon was held at the picturesque Sandpiper Inn on a point overlooking the Atlantic Ocean. After lunch, we drove to the church in Rockport for our small, simple, yet beautiful wedding ceremony.

After we returned to Miami, Muffin's parents hosted a huge outdoor reception for us at their home on Hammock Lake. My parents, Roselle and Arthur Bell, attended the reception even though they were unable to make the long trip to Boston for the wedding because of my father's health. After the reception, my father went to a guest bedroom to rest. My mother, Muffin, and I were visiting later in the kitchen when a torrential rainstorm suddenly started. Muffin and I spontaneously shouted in unison, "The table!" A very nice large wooden table was left outside after the reception. Without another word, Muffin and I bolted outside together at top speed to save the table from the rain. We instantly lifted it as one and rapidly moved it inside. Watching in amazement, my mother commented, "Why, there is hardly a drop of water on the table, and you guys didn't even get wet! I never saw a couple work together so well and move so fast. If I hadn't seen it for myself, I wouldn't have believed it!"

I always recalled with pride my mother's comments that night. Muffin's reflexes were incredibly fast, but now she was dead, and I was all alone in my painful struggle. Our perfect partnership in this life was now completely gone with only my treasured memories of Muffin remaining. I finally fell asleep for the night, dreaming of our life together.

CHAPTER 6
ACUPUNCTURE BY ACCIDENT

When I woke up the next morning, my overall condition was stabilizing. My mother helped get me moved from ICU to a regular private room in the hospital. This opened the door for visitors.

As I was getting settled in my room, Muffin's Uncle Bill came by and asked if I needed anything? "Yes," I pleaded, "please bring me some real food from outside the hospital. A large salad would be great." He soon appeared with a huge homemade salad from Aunt Pat, enough to last for a few days! The salad was absolutely divine, and I had not eaten any real food for two long, agonizing days. I sat up in bed with the very large salad bowl and ate the entire salad to the muted amusement of an appreciative audience. The room was packed with relatives, and they along with the interaction of my visitors helped puncture the gloom in the room.

My gargantuan eating feat lightened the mood of everyone including me. They "could not believe he ate the whole thing," especially Uncle Bill who brought the salad. I was cheering up some in the midst of the overall ordeal, and my visitors were more cheerful now as they continued their efforts to comfort and console me. At this moment, a plastic surgeon appeared unexpectedly in the doorway of my hospital room. Hesitantly, he asked, "Is it okay if I come in? I am making some rounds at the hospital, and I decided to check on you to see how you are doing."

I responded, "Come on in, doctor. Thank you for taking care of me."

He looked at his work on my face and head and reminded me to go to his office when I get out of the hospital. Then he would rough up some of the skin grafts so I would not have as much scarring. He looked at my swollen forehead on the right side of my head. "I see you still have a pretty bad concussion. Do you mind if I drill a little hole in your head to relieve some of the pressure and help bring the swelling down?"

I heard jokes all my life about having a hole in your head. I'll have to admit I never received such an unusual request from a doctor on the spur of the moment, especially as there was no advance information or discussion. I was thinking this was outside his specialty, but I was open to trying anything to get some relief.

"Go right *a-head*, doctor. No pun intended."

He looked surprised I was trying to lighten the atmosphere in the room. I wasn't really trying to be comical. I often say things like that. Sometimes it turns out to be funny, and often the joke is on me, but it helps me relieve stress and try to put others at ease even though it may be at my own expense. That's just who I am. It's part of my personality, thinking of catchy phrases to label special situations.

The doctor left the room without saying anything, and I feared he might be offended by what I said. He soon returned with his little black bag. He took out a small hand drill operated by turning a tiny flywheel, similar to an old-fashioned, manually operated egg beater. My head was sensitive, but it was somewhat numbed from the concussion. The drilling hurt some, but what made it worse was the annoying, whining, grinding noise it made.

Suddenly, the drill broke through my skull, and the pressure from the concussion was instantly relieved. At the same time I realized I could miraculously now move both legs. I joyously yelled, "I'm not paralyzed anymore," and cried. Applause and celebration broke out. This was a major milestone on my road to recovery as promised by the angel, and everyone wanted to hear some good news. There was too much bad news about us.

The doctor explained sometimes strange things happen when working around the head or face because there are so many nerves. Without thinking I automatically commented in amazement, "It must be acupuncture by accident." Everyone in the room laughed. Even the doctor laughed nervously. I wasn't trying to be funny. I was just trying to comprehend and possibly explain the apparently miraculous situation that suddenly occurred as swiftly as a lightning strike.

Even though I could now move my arms and legs, I was still in intense pain. I could not walk, but now I felt I really had a chance to regain my mobility even though the doctors initially told me I would never walk again. The plastic surgeon left my room with a sense of satisfaction as I repeatedly expressed my deep gratitude to him for miraculously relieving my paralysis.

Soon after he left my room, a tall, stately young woman with perfect posture stood in the doorway. She was well-dressed but not fancy in her summer clothes. The weather in South Florida in July is very hot and humid. The lady made direct eye contact with me with the same penetrating gaze as the angel. I recognized her as the Good Samaritan who stopped at the scene of the accident and placed the strangely printed beach towel over me. Without breaking her penetrating gaze, she asked me if I was okay. "Are you sure?" she asked. I said again that I was okay. Still locked in direct eye contact with me, she responded, "Well, if you are sure you are okay and don't need anything, I'll go."

Before she walked away, I asked her for her name and telephone number so I could contact her later to thank her. She scribbled a name and number on a piece of torn scrap paper and said the number was her work number. I thanked her again, and she left.

I had the strangest sense if Elizabeth was grown up, she might look like this lady. I wondered if I had just encountered another guardian angel as she seemed to have authority and possibly even power to help me as she stood poised to respond to my needs. Several weeks later, I found the piece of paper with my stuff from the hospital, and I attempted to contact her. To my surprise I was told no one with her name had ever worked there. She disappeared without a trace. I thought maybe my mind was playing tricks on me, except when my personal belongings were returned to me upon leaving the hospital, the unearthly looking beach towel was with my possessions from the night of the wreck.

I kept the beach towel for another twenty years through several moves until it finally disappeared. Neither I nor anyone in my family knows what happened to that towel... or to that lady.

After the plastic surgeon and the mysterious lady left, I was really ready to get some rest. The next morning I would start physical therapy. Tomorrow evening would be the wake for Muffin and Elizabeth at the Elliotts' home. I would need as much rest and strength as I could muster to endure the next day. For now, I was confined to my hospital bed all alone with my anger and grief as I fell asleep totally exhausted.

CHAPTER 7
SHOCK OF WHITE

The next morning, I was taken to therapy and placed in the Hubbard water tank on my back on a slanted board to prevent my head from going underwater. Although my motion in the water was very limited, it was still acutely painful. I was making progress, and the therapists and doctors were satisfied with my first efforts. After therapy, I returned to my room for a late lunch and rest.

Late afternoon, my brother-in-law Bay Elliott came to help me get dressed for the wake in the evening. He checked me out of the hospital in my wheelchair. I don't remember many details about that afternoon.

I sat in shock in my wheelchair next to the one closed casket holding the bodies of both Muffin and Elizabeth and greeted many friends and family members who came.

Beside the casket on a large easel was a beautiful enlarged color photograph of Muffin and Elizabeth from the previous Christmas dinner hosted by Uncle Don and Aunt Carole at the Riviera Country in Coral Gables. Both Muffin and Elizabeth looked radiant in their best dresses. There were beautiful flowers arranged around the photograph.

I was feeling overwhelming grief and searing physical pain. I could no longer endure greeting the long line of people who came to show their sympathy and support. As I was about to collapse, my dear friends Frank and Jan Barry from New Orleans walked through the door. They had flown in to be with me. They were true friends. Their arrival and encouragement helped me get through the rest of the wake. Later that night, Bay returned me to my hospital room where I slept all alone.

The memorial service the next morning at Plymouth Congregational Church in Coconut Grove was packed with a mass of people. Mrs. Elliott spoke lovingly about Muffin's life and faith and her certainty that Muffin and Elizabeth were now in Heaven. Mrs. Elliott described Muffin's life of service to others including her counseling work at the Henderson Mental Health Clinic in Fort Lauderdale. Elizabeth's babysitter, Juli Cabrera, told about Elizabeth and her fun-loving, captivating personality. One of my older sisters, Martha Blackburn from Valdosta, Georgia, came and encouraged me after the service.

Many of those who attended the memorial service said that it was positive, uplifting, and an inspiring statement of faith in spite of the terrible tragedy. The love and support of friends and family there helped me deal with staggering, paralyzing grief, and the service strengthened my faith.

At the cemetery, the burial plot was next to a building with a beautiful reflecting pool, providing a sense of calm and peace. After the service, as I sat in my wheelchair, friends and family came up to speak to me again. Some began asking me if my hair was white before the wreck or if it turned white because of the loss of Muffin and Elizabeth. I was too preoccupied to notice a change in my hair color. Before the accident, my hair was dark brown with some specks of black, but after the agonizing grief of the preceding hours and days, it had suddenly turned white.

As Bay drove me back to the hospital again, I asked him about my hair color. He told me he noticed my hair suddenly turned white, but he did not want to upset me more than I already was by mentioning it.

I thanked Bay for helping me get dressed two days in a row and for taking me where I needed to be. Then it was time for me to rest in my hospital room, alone again! I needed to be ready for more grueling therapy in the days and weeks ahead, but I was unable to sleep. I was again struggling with grief.

CHAPTER 8
CHILD OF PROMISE

As I lay awake asking myself over and over again why and how things could have been different, I agonized over the loss of Elizabeth, stuck down at such an early age while she was showing such great promise going forward. Now her special future in this life would never happen.

Muffin and I worked hard to advance our careers—she, in psychiatric social work; me, in my legal career. We always wanted children. When we were ready to start our family, we confronted difficulties. After consulting with doctors, Muffin used a doctor-prescribed fertility drug and became pregnant in 1980. After several months, Muffin woke up one night in terrible pain. At the hospital, she suffered a miscarriage of an unborn son.

We were in shock and thoroughly devastated. It was painful to be with the young children of our family and friends. We desperately wanted our own children. Now we were just casual observers of the joys of other parents with their children. After Muffin regained her health, we decided to try again. Muffin became pregnant a second time in 1981. Although we experienced many nervous moments during the monitoring of her pregnancy, we were successful! Elizabeth was born at South Miami Hospital on January 18, 1982, at 8:34 p.m. She weighed 8 pounds, 14 and ½ ounces. Her full name was Rosalie Elizabeth Bell, the fifth generation of Rosalies on Muffin's side of the family. The name Elizabeth came from my side of the family, after my great-great grandmother Elizabeth, who reared her sons by herself in the 1840s after the death of her husband. Her full name honored strong women on both sides of our family.

Almost immediately, Elizabeth showed great promise and determination. She made strong eye contact with everyone she met. Her fun, playful smile brightened the entire room. Everyone anywhere near her began smiling, too. Her contagious personality engaged others wherever we went. Muffin and I soon realized we were simply known as "Elizabeth's parents." She was so well-behaved and so delightful to be around that we were especially welcome in the homes of family and friends if we had Elizabeth with us!

In June, 1984, we returned from another trip to Europe, combining both business and pleasure. While we were in London, I met with my bosses at Lloyd's of London in the Underwriters' Claims Office, while Muffin and Elizabeth enjoyed shopping on Oxford Street, the Haymarket, Knightsbridge, and elsewhere in London. Even though Elizabeth was just two years, five months old, she enjoyed London immensely. She and Muffin attended the afternoon High Tea at Fortnum and Mason department store, where Elizabeth stood up on her chair in her pretty little fluffy dress and sang the "Now I Know My ABC's" song perfectly, showing an early talent for singing. The mostly well-dressed, older ladies in attendance spontaneously applauded in unison. Elizabeth was like a little sparkler, igniting enjoyment and entertainment for everyone around her.

Elizabeth played very well with children of all ages. When we visited Muffin's sister Audrey and her husband Christian who lived in a small village in the Lake District of Austria near Salzburg, Elizabeth somehow learned to communicate with the local children (kinders) who played nearby. As Audrey's husband was a doctor who practiced in a clinic in part of their home, there was an abundance of locals for Elizabeth to charm with her endearing, energetic personality.

After we returned from our trip overseas, Elizabeth developed an independent streak common to all budding toddlers. If we offered to help her with anything, she would usually say with an air of determination and grit: "I want to do it **by myself.**" When she completed her activity to her satisfaction, she would exclaim emphatically, "**Now.**" to mark her success.

Because Elizabeth was the "star" of the show, it was not unusual to take her with us to North Miami that night.… Now there was only horrible heartbreak and haunting hints of what might have been if normal activities had been different that night. I finally fell fitfully asleep for the night in pain focused on my treasured memories of my magnetic daughter and her contagious charm.

Muffin, Elizabeth and Bob Chistmas, 1983

Elizabeth dancing with grandfather E.B. Elliott as
grandmother Rosalie Elliott enjoys watching

Muffin holding baby Elizabeth

CHAPTER 9

FIRST STEPS

In the morning, I was taken to therapy and placed on a slanted board in the water tank. My movement was better with less pain, and I was lowered deeper into the water at a sharper angle. This allowed me to move my arms and legs more freely without placing my weight on them although it was still painful. After an extended time, I was cut loose from the restraints keeping me on the board. I floated and moved around in the water without too much pain. Before the wreck, I was a good swimmer, taking the drown-proofing course at Emory University and earlier qualifying as a Scout Lifeguard with the Boy Scouts. The therapist and doctors were satisfied with my progress at the end of that session, and I was returned alone to my room.

In my hospital bed, I started thinking about what the angel said about bringing the pickup truck driver to justice and locating witnesses. I would need a top-notch lawyer with a very good investigator as I was helpless. I could not walk and was in intense pain. I could not type or write because I was right-handed. My right elbow was fractured and needed time to heal.

I thought about what Muffin would want me to do. She had a friend, Sophia, with a young son Daniel who was a frequent playmate with Elizabeth. Sophia was originally from The Netherlands and was married to a very reputable, very experienced injury attorney, Steve Tarr. I met Steve once at a small family party, and I enjoyed talking with him. Muffin told me one of Steve's older sons wanted to do graduate work at Emory and needed a grant to make it possible. Muffin promised Sophia that I would help obtain a grant for Steve's son. Muffin thought I was very well connected, but I was baffled as to how to obtain a grant for Steve's son at Emory even though I graduated from college and law school there.

If I hired Steve as my lawyer, that would help me and his family. I asked for a telephone as I did not have enough mobility to get it for myself, and I could not reach it. I was confined to my hospital bed unless I had assistance. Steve was very surprised that I was calling him from my hospital bed and even more surprised that I wanted him to immediately come to the hospital to sign papers for him to represent me. At first Steve politely declined, saying, "I am not an ambulance chaser, and I do not want to look like an ambulance chaser. We can meet when you are in better shape after you get out of the hospital."

Remembering what the angel said about locating witnesses, I told Steve, "This cannot wait. We need to get your investigator working now to locate witnesses. It may be too late by the time I get out of the hospital. You must come to the hospital now so that we can get started without delay doing what needs to be done." When Steve realized I was alert and serious, he reluctantly agreed to come to the hospital. When he arrived several hours later, he was organized for business. He talked with me, and his investigator took photographs of my injuries. He said they would get to work right away locating witnesses and investigating the wreck, but we would wait to sign the representation contract when I was out of the hospital and not taking pain-killing medicine.

After Steve left, I still had the telephone on my bed. I asked for help again to dial another number. I called my office and spoke to Betty. At first, she thought it was a call about how I was doing. After we talked about my condition and some progress I made, I told her I wanted to dictate to her on the new, big tuna fish shipping claim. She was shocked and asked me if I was serious. "Shouldn't you be resting? Are you sure you are well enough to dictate? What about all the medicine you are taking?" I said, "Betty, you know my work. You know about this claim. You know we need to arrest this ship or obtain security for the claim from the vessel's insurer. Let me dictate these letters, and if they sound OK, send them out! If they sound garbled like I am on drugs, hold them until they can be corrected later."

I dictated a letter to Jeremy Thomas, a lawyer I knew and trusted in London, asking him to find the ship and threaten to arrest it so the vessel's insurer in London would post a bond to keep the vessel free from seizure. I dictated another letter to my client in San Francisco reporting that the vessel was being actively pursued to obtain security for the claim. This would let the client know I was still in business and taking care of the claim. If the vessel escaped, the large claim would be virtually uncollectible. By now I was very tired and left everything in Betty's hands. I rested somewhat better that night and slept more soundly until morning.

The next morning I thought I was being taken back to the water tank for more therapy, but when I got there, I was told I had graduated from the water tank. I was stood up between two parallel hand railings in the therapy area. It was painful being taken out of my wheelchair and placed in that position, and it was painful just standing there. Then I was told to try to walk. This was ridiculous. I could not even move my feet. They said I had to start somewhere if I was going to walk again. I can't tell you how much it hurt or how much I gritted my teeth, groaned, and grunted as I struggled to move my left foot forward because that was my better side.

Finally, my left foot moved less than one inch forward. I repeated this movement and dragged my right foot along slightly. The therapist encouraged me to keep trying. By the end of the lengthy session, I was very slowly taking steps of one inch or more. There was excruciating pain in my pelvic area that was limiting my motion. Every tiny forward movement of my feet produced terrible pain in my pelvic area and lower back.

The following day was more of the same, but I decided to use pain constructively to manage and measure my progress. If the pain was too much, I would temporarily back off. I would push to my pain limit so I could gradually increase the prior limits of my mobility. This approach started showing results. While holding onto the parallel hand railings, I was moving my feet between two and three inches each time. I worked my way all along the parallel hand railings from one end to the other and started over again in the opposite direction. Two doctors watched, and one of them commented, "You sure are in a hurry. You are moving right along, wasting no time." I responded, "You lose it if you don't use it. After thirty days my muscles will begin to atrophy if I don't regain their use." The doctor said, "That's right, but who told you?" I said, "I don't know, but I heard that, and I believe it's true."

After I was returned in my wheelchair to my room, I called Betty. She sent the letters. She said they were OK, that she only needed to clarify a few words. I was very tired again and rested and slept until the next day. I thought I was getting into a therapy routine to be repeated day after day. I was looking forward to tomorrow in hopes I could work on lengthening my stride. Before the wreck I had a very long stride, and others had difficulty keeping up with me when we were walking together.

CHAPTER 10
NO PAIN KILLERS

The next morning, I was surprised to learn I was leaving the hospital. On Saturday the doctors wanted to get me out of the hospital for the weekend after almost a week and a half there, and I was happy to depart. I received the best treatment after they decided not to let me die, but it was time to return to a more normal environment. I was still in a wheelchair when I was picked up from the hospital. The plan was to go to the Elliotts' home where I could continue therapy in their swimming pool, and I was taken there in one of the Elliotts' cars.

We discussed how to use their swimming pool for therapeutic exercise. It had steps at the shallow end where I could roll my wheelchair up to the top step, put on the brakes and lower myself out of the wheelchair down to the top step. Using my arms again, from there I could lower myself down one step at a time until I was in the water, touching bottom without putting much weight on my feet or legs. I would float or swim softly while getting gentle exercise. In the water I felt almost weightless. I was OK unless someone moved the wheelchair at the top step before I got out of the water.

Rosalie Elliott asked if my pain killers were beginning to wear off as I appeared to become more uncomfortable. Then she asked, "Where are your pain killers?" We looked everywhere, but there were no pain killers. We realized I had left the hospital without any pain killers and without any prescriptions for pain killers. With my increasing pain and no drugs, a call was quickly placed to the hospital, but the doctors had gone home for the weekend. The hospital personnel were told this situation is absolutely unacceptable, but they told us no prescriptions could be written for me because I was no longer a patient at the hospital. We tried not to yell and scream at the hospital workers, but it was clear I was now on my own in the worst way.

I remembered Vitamin C is a natural muscle relaxer, and Rosalie Elliott had 1,500 milligram 12-hour time release Vitamin C tablets. I immediately took one of these tablets along with two aspirins and repeated this combined dose every morning and evening after that. This provided an increasing amount of relief from pain, and my physical condition was also gradually improving with increased exercise in the swimming pool. I was able to roll my wheelchair up to the shower enclosure and stand up inside the shower, leaning against the wall or holding onto a wall fixture. If I dropped the soap bar, I could not pick it up because I could not bend over or bend my knees enough to reach it. I used a soap-on-a-rope around my neck so I could take showers and get myself clean.

On Monday, I decided to stick with the vitamins and aspirins and forget the drugs. I did not want to become addicted to pain killers, and now I had a way out if I stayed the course. I continued to use pain constructively to manage and measure my daily progress, pushing to my limit each time but being careful not to re-injure myself by pushing too far at one time. Therapy was a gradual step-by-step process for me, constantly improving in small increments but fortunately usually not slipping backward.

While I was still at the Elliotts', Steve Tarr came by with the legal papers for me to sign. He was acting as my attorney and also as a friend. He told me I should read the Book of Job in the Bible, and I read it often in the years following the wreck. I finally understood the lesson from Job. He was restored when he prayed for his friends who had blamed him for his suffering, and Job really knew how to pray for others because of his own troubles.

Staying with the Elliotts helped me more than I could ever say, but I needed to get back to my house and my office. Sooner or later, I would have to face the empty house without Muffin and Elizabeth, and I needed to get back to work. My office was in a separate area of the house with a separate entrance at the other end of the building from the residential rooms. This was an arrangement I heard about from my brother-in-law Dr. Christian when he came to Miami from Austria to marry Audrey. The Elliotts' home was a protective shelter for me in my angry, painful, disabled condition, but I needed to return to my house to confront the dual challenges of missing my family and my lingering work responsibilities that were growing daily. The longer I waited, the more difficult it would be.

CHAPTER 11
HIDING A HANDICAP

I went home with my wheelchair, but the Elliotts worried about me. They asked me to stay out of the office and take more time to rest and recover. My mother went back to her home in Cairo, Georgia, and I was alone in the house except when there was work in the office. Betty tried to keep me out of the office, believing it was best for me, but I could not be away from the office. My work was all that was left. I managed to reach the office in my wheelchair, lifting myself across four split levels to get there. I went no farther than my desk that was in the first room of the office. I struggled out of my wheelchair and into the executive chair behind my desk. Suddenly, I felt no pain for the first time since the wreck. I had found the only place where I did not hurt. I was comfortable in my own chair.

I began to do the work on my desk. I lasted forty-five minutes before I was too tired to continue. I got into my wheelchair and returned to the far end of the house to deal with my injuries and fatigue, but now I knew I would be back, gradually increasing the time I could work. When I was completely alone, I was overcome by my anger that Muffin and Elizabeth were not there. I yelled at God, "If you don't want them, send them back to me!" Instead of being struck down by God, a strong, unusual sense of calm and peace came over me. I realized again what I had seen in the encounter with the angel was true. Muffin and Elizabeth were with God in Heaven. After that I was not angry toward God. I realized how much he was helping me in spite of my tragedies. I thought about the encounter with the angel, wondering when and how the predictions about the future would come true in my lifetime.

I was having trouble with the wheelchair because of the multiple split levels. I decided to try a walker. It was difficult and painful at first, but it was better than the wheelchair. I knew I had to drive again as soon as possible to get past the fear of driving caused by the wreck. While fighting fear, I needed food! I struggled to get into the car and drove to the nearby Publix grocery store at Suniland. I realized I was driving the Buick again before I could walk. I thought the other shoppers at Publix would be sympathetic, but they treated me with disdain, looked the other way, and acted impatient for me and my walker to get out of their way. They treated me like trash that should be swept out of sight. I began to realize what I was up against. I started to notice that handicap parking spaces were often not the closest to the entrance. Parking spaces for the handicapped were often located to the detriment of the disabled, leaving the best parking for normal, healthy individuals who are the pride of the people.

I realized if the other lawyers ("sharks") knew how disabled and incapacitated I was they could put me away competitively. They could schedule numerous depositions I could not attend including out of town or foreign locations. They could bury me with paperwork. I could only work two hours each day. They could schedule multiple hearings on simple motions instead of agreeing and default me at every opportunity, knowing I was especially vulnerable. I developed a strategy to hide my handicap and convince everyone I was OK. While I was thinking about how to implement my plan, I received some good news on the big tuna fish shipping claim. Jeremy Thomas had obtained a guarantee of coverage from the ship's insurer in London to avoid the vessel's seizure and detention in a foreign port. Now the large claim would be collectible. We would not be wasting time or money in pursuing the claim.

Driven by fear as a handicapped person of being kicked while I was down, I managed to walk again without a walker six weeks after the wreck. I could take only short, choppy steps, and I could walk only straight forward and a little straight back. I could not turn or maneuver on my feet in a normal manner. If

I accidentally dropped something, I could not reach down and pick it up. If anyone saw me walking, they would know I was a sitting duck. I had to hide my handicap at all costs! If I had no way to earn a living, surviving my injuries would be less significant.

In August, in Miami after the wreck in July, the courts were not busy because of vacations. After Labor Day, court hearings started to be scheduled in September. I decided to pre-position myself in the Courtroom. I went early when no one was there and sat down up front. Then I stayed put. When my case was called, I simply stood up. When my case was over, I sat down and busied myself working on my notes. When the Courtroom was empty after everyone left, I lumbered out, trying to be careful not to be seen by anyone who might recognize me. I heard later the word was spreading among the lawyers that I was OK, that I was doing amazingly well after the wreck that killed my wife and daughter. The lawyers who had direct contact with me had apparently decided I was not a target of opportunity, that tangling with me would probably not be rewarding.

My plan was working well, and I later did the same thing with Navy receptions in Washington. I went very early, stayed in one spot, and left after everyone was gone. I heard there was talk about me among the Navy officers about how well I was doing after the wreck. I was apparently performing my duties without any problems. I was seen as OK.

I went back to the cemetery several times in the process of making arrangements for memorial markers for Muffin and Elizabeth. I wanted military markers with the cross because we were a military and a Christian family. When the markers were completed, I continued to visit the cemetery. On one of my regular visits to the cemetery, I heard a Voice saying, "Why seek ye the living among the dead?" I kept driving toward the cemetery, but as I got closer to the cemetery, the Voice got increasingly louder and kept repeating the same question from Scripture. "Why seek ye the living among the dead?" I finally got the message, turned the car around and went home.

God was telling me again Muffin and Elizabeth *are* alive with Him in Heaven just as I saw at the wreck during the encounter with the angel. This was the third time God reassured me including the time I was overcome with anger when I returned home alone after the wreck. After hearing the Voice that kept me from going to the cemetery, I did not need further assurance. I recalled the Scripture that to be absent from the body is to be present with the Lord. (2 Cor. 5:8 New International Version)

After I stopped visiting the cemetery, I was not grieving as much outwardly, but I was just grieving differently, going to my memories of them when they were alive on earth and knowing they *are* alive in Heaven forever. I continued to miss them terribly, but I knew I should not dwell in despair. They would want me to live for something as the angel told me during the encounter. I should focus on surviving and recovering from my injuries so I could work on my missions from the encounter.

Grieving sometimes involves contact with many individuals and group activities. Sometimes it is the opposite, seeking seclusion. With me it was some of both, but my bereavement was more "uncomplicated" because of my encounter with the angel, giving me the will to live, new purpose in life, and assurance of eternal salvation.

CHAPTER 12
STAYING IN THE NAVY

The encounter with the angel changed my plans about staying in the Navy. I was in a reserve status so I had time to fulfill my performance requirements. My July weekend reserve drills were performed before the wreck on July 19. I was excused from the August reserve drills I could perform later as make-up drills. I was appointed before the wreck effective October 1, 1984 as Commanding Officer of a reserve legal unit assisting the Military Justice Division of the Office of the Judge Advocate General of the Navy in Washington. Now I was afraid my command could be given to someone else because of my injuries.

I was upset because I received orders for active duty in Seattle in July. Those orders were cancelled after I was appointed Commanding Officer of the Washington, D.C. unit. If we had been in Seattle, the wreck in Miami could not have occurred. I struggled to put those painful thoughts about Seattle out of my mind. I decided to prove I could still perform my duties well. I applied for two weeks active duty in Washington during the second half of September to close out the current government fiscal year followed by another two weeks of active duty in the first half of October in the new fiscal year to meet requirements in both years. I was determined to show the Navy I was not washed up. I could command.

The first two weeks were very painful with the walking, but I stayed in a motel next to the government office building in Alexandria, Virginia where I was working. I was still taking huge doses of Vitamin C with aspirin, and I took extra aspirin. After the first two weeks, I was doing much better. Being forced to walk almost everywhere helped me progress faster in my physical recovery. Receiving comments from my Navy bosses about "job well done" boosted my spirits and my confidence. When I left Washington in the middle of October after four weeks, I was ready to command the reserve unit and bring them to Washington to assist with the military justice cases and reviews. I developed a plan to better utilize reserve unit personnel in direct support of the full-time active duty staff, actually helping them with their case loads.

As most lawyers and legal personnel have somewhat flexible schedules, I planned to combine two monthly reserve weekends for four days in Washington, arriving Thursday evening for work Friday through Monday. The third monthly reserve weekend of the three months Quarter would be at the home reserve center in Miami for needed activity there. This cut the government's travel costs in half compared to two separate reserve weekends in Washington. We were given work assignments by active duty personnel when we reported for work Friday morning. We worked on these assignments through the weekend and submitted the completed work to active duty staff before flying home Monday evening. Productivity soared. The backlog of military justice cases was quickly reduced. My plan was approved by the regional reserve Admiral in Jacksonville, Florida and by the Judge Advocate General of the Navy. My plan was widely copied by other Navy Reserve legal units and by many non-legal reserve units.

During the early months of 1985, my command was secured in spite of my injuries and tragic family deaths. My birthday was December 22, and my Annual Navy Physical was due in January, but it was re-scheduled to February. By then I could pass the physical exam. I was able to do my job as a Navy lawyer and lead my reserve unit to greater accomplishments.

A miraculous transformation occurred in seven months from "basket case" to a more effective and determined leader. It was clear that I would be staying in the Navy. From planning only two more years to complete my twenty years for retirement, I was now embarked on a different course. My reserve unit command had been planned as a "twilight tour," completing twenty years of service and then retiring with my command as my concluding achievement that I had worked for twenty years to reach and complete before "going over the hill into the sunset." Now, I was committed to staying in the Navy "for the duration" for as long as possible. I thought about the encounter with the angel and the Grace of God that brought me back to life, healed me, and transformed me into a more effective and dedicated Navy officer and leader. I wondered what else was in the future that the angel alluded to and how would I "know what it is when the time comes?"

CHAPTER 13
THE CRIMINAL CASE

Meanwhile, the criminal case dragged on with the defendant in custody. He said he was a first offender. He said I was driving on the wrong side of the road and caused the wreck, but he had a very high level of alcohol and drugs in his blood when he was tested not long after the wreck. He was arrested by the Florida Marine Patrol. He was driving without a valid driver's license, without a valid tag and registration for his pickup truck, without insurance, and with his high-beam headlights on. He was driving home from a bar when the wreck occurred.

He had one prior arrest in Florida on a traffic stop when he was driving without insurance, but he was almost immediately released on his claim that he had no prior record when the arresting officers checked and could not find any record of prior offenses. When he came from out of state and obtained a Florida driver's license, he said he had no prior record. His Florida license was suspended at the time of the wreck because he had not provided evidence of insurance as required after his previous Florida traffic stop. The angel said the defendant did a lot of bad things and was to be brought to justice. I did not believe he had no prior record. How could his prior record be found? Everyone who checked was missing it.

While this mystery concerning the defendant's prior record existed for months, it was necessary to take my deposition. I testified that the collision's impact knocked our small car against and slightly past the center line at one spot. We were definitely driving on the right side of the road when we were hit. Then it was necessary to go to the Court Reporter's Office to make corrections as there were obvious errors in the transcript. After that, the deposition of the only known independent eyewitness was taken, but he was listed on the police report as a bystander, someone who stopped after the accident to help if possible.

Steve Tarr's investigator was very thorough. He contacted everyone who was listed on the police report, whether listed as a witness or not. In talking with this man, the investigator learned he was driving his pickup truck north on Biscayne Boulevard in the opposite direction from where the wreck occurred. He had already passed the location of the wreck when the collision occurred. That's why the police said he was not a witness because he was facing away and driving away from the place of impact when the wreck happened, but this man told the investigator something very important. There was a very bright flash of light in the sky behind him that caused him to look in his rear-view mirror. He was horrified to see the wreck very clearly in his rear-view mirror *as it was happening.*

He testified that our car was on the right side of the road and that the defendant's pickup truck crossed the center line of the road at full speed and hit our small car head on. The angel was right again!! The only known independent eyewitness would never have been located if I had not lived and hired Steve Tarr who sent his investigator out to look for witnesses. If I had died, there would not have been any witnesses, not even me. The defendant could have said anything to get away with what he did without being refuted.

As the case continued to drag on for more months, the lack of a prior record for the defendant troubled me. It did not fit with other known facts. It did not fit with what the angel said, but where was the proof? Around this time I was conferring with Steve Tarr about the insurance claims. He told me I had twice as much auto insurance coverage as I thought. Because the defendant had no insurance, the injury and death claims would go against my uninsured motorist coverage that was twice as much as I realized.

Now I was reluctant to challenge the angel on such an obviously incorrect fact, but Steve Tarr was not an angel, although a human guardian angel for me. I said, "Steve, that's ridiculous. I know how much coverage I purchased. It's only half of what you are saying." He replied, "Wait a minute. Let me tell you something. The Florida courts have a rule that allows you to stack coverage based upon the number of cars that you insured. You had two cars that were insured, and so you multiply two times the amount of coverage that you purchased to get your adjusted total. That's stacking, and it means you have twice as much uninsured motorist coverage as you realized." I thought, "Chalk up another one for the angel." Then I said to myself, "There must be a prior record somewhere. The angel has always been right."

My first major mission from the angel to help bring the defendant to justice was floundering without the defendant's prior record, even with the factual testimony from me and the independent eyewitness who was discovered after he was overlooked by the police. As a first offender, the defendant would probably receive lenient treatment under the sentencing guidelines. In the absence of a prior record, the defendant was pleading not guilty, and there was no guarantee he would be convicted if the case went to trial. There would be no sentencing without a conviction or a guilty plea.

CHAPTER 14
THE EUROPA CAFÉ

In early December, 1984, I went to New York City to meet with representatives of some insurance companies about claims I was handling. I contacted my Navy friends there who were JAG's. They were very concerned about me and were glad I was back at work in New York City before the holidays. I was there so many times on business I was almost an honorary resident of New York City. Three of my Navy JAG friends, Lee Fuller, Bob Lunney, and Larry Brennan invited me for lunch. Speaking for all three, Lee Fuller said, "We just want to talk with you to find out how you are doing to see if there is anything we can do for you. We will take you to lunch at a different place that you do not know to make it interesting. Meet us at The Europa Café over on the East side of Midtown."

I did not know how to find The Europa Café, but the taxi driver took me there right away from The University Club where I was staying. When I arrived, my three friends already had a table in a quiet corner and were waiting for me. The restaurant was not busy that day, and there was no rush. This was one of the best things that happened for me after the wreck and was a tremendous boost to my spirits. I felt almost normal to be with good friends, almost as if nothing had changed, but then the conversation turned to my troubles. They were concerned for me as friends. They asked about the criminal case, and as lawyers their questions went beyond general interest. They wanted to know the exact status and the details of each aspect of the case. They wanted the case to go forward correctly.

I said the defendant was from out of state and claimed to have no prior criminal record. Nothing had been found so far to show any prior record. They asked me where he was before coming to Florida. I said he was in the border area of Connecticut and New York on the edge of the New York City Metropolitan Area. They said, "Hey, we know the State Assembly Representative from that area of New York, and we will ask him to look into it." I said, "Please do," and thanked them. Now it was time to get back to work, and the conversation turned to farewells and best wishes for the coming holidays. As we were leaving, I said I hoped to see them in Florida before the cold weather was over in New York. We parted as friends until we met again.

I walked back to The University Club to help my progress toward recovery, and I wanted to remember where The Europa Café was located so I find it again. The Europa Café was associated in my mind with good friends, a good time, and good intentions expressed by true friends. I did not know if they would find out anything about the defendant in New York, but now there was some hope. My friends asked me to keep them informed about the progress of the case on the Court's Calendar, and I did. After our lunch at The Europa Café, nothing happened for two months as the Court date in February was fast approaching. The defendant was still in custody but had pleaded not guilty and was asking for a jury trial. No prior record had been found, and the case was put on the Court's Trial Calendar in February, 1985.

I wondered if the angel had finally missed something. It did not seem possible that he could be wrong, but on the issue of a prior record, there was a deafening silence stretching over seven months. There was nothing about any prior offenses or arrests before Florida, and family and friends were preparing to come to court with me on the appointed day to seek justice.

CHAPTER 15
HOME AWAY FROM HOME FOR THE HOLIDAYS

Returning from New York, the painful reality of the first Christmas and New Year's without Muffin and Elizabeth was like a huge anchor dragging me down. I needed a real break with a change of locale to survive. I also had to face the challenging reality of taking timely action on my workload to keep my livelihood. From working forty-five minutes each day after the wreck, I increased to two hours and then four hours each day, but I needed to do more. The most pressing large claim was the frozen tuna fish shipment delivered damaged in Italy.

Jeremy Thomas obtained security for the claim, and it was submitted to Arbitration at London through the Maritime Arbitrators Association. The United States District Court in San Juan, Puerto Rico retained jurisdiction, but because of arbitration clauses in the shipping contracts, the case was referred to Arbitration at London for assessment of responsibility and damages. Then the Arbitrator's Award could be enforced through the Court in San Juan.

I needed to quickly take statements of witnesses in Italy for the Arbitration at London. The client was ready to proceed, and the client's representative from San Diego, California made arrangements to meet me in Milan, Italy on January 2, 1985. Appointments were scheduled with key witnesses in Italy. The ship was chartered to carry the cargo of frozen tuna fish from Mayaguez, Puerto Rico to Genoa, Italy for processing at a cannery in Italy where much of the fish was found to be not fit for human consumption because of refrigeration failure in transit.

Getting to Milan for January 2 was challenging. Because of the time difference, travel time, airline schedules and availability of flights during the holiday period, I had to already be there on January 2 ready for work. Muffin's sister Audrey and her husband Christian invited me to spend the holidays with them in their village near Salzburg, Austria. I could travel to Austria to stay with them during the holidays before taking a short early morning flight on New Year's Day from Vienna across the Alps down to Milan. I would be in Milan on January 2 for an early start on the witness statements. This was a God thing. I would get the rest, relaxation, and recovery time I desperately needed to be able to do my job. If I didn't go to Austria for the holidays, I could not get to work in Milan on time.

My mother was not happy, but she understood. She wanted me to spend Christmas with her at home in Cairo, Georgia. My dad, Arthur died in November, 1982, and she did not want to be alone, so she made plans with some other family members. We would be preoccupied with agonizing thoughts and discussions about the wreck if we were together. That would not be good for either of us. God was giving both of us a much needed break so we could take care of ourselves. God was orchestrating situations to relieve much of the oppressive stress in our lives with the deaths of family members followed by more trouble.

I was preparing to leave for Austria, but there was still no prior record on the defendant. There was no reason not to believe the angel. He was correct about everything so far. Possibly we were just failing to find the prior record although it was out there somewhere. It must exist in routine records, but where was it? I could not do anything else until I returned from Europe in January, two and a half weeks later. I had to concentrate on the tasks involved in the trip to Europe and allow myself to rest and recuperate mentally and physically. I was totally exhausted. I was burned out mentally and beat up physically.

I took a flight to New York and transferred at JFK International Airport onto a flight to Frankfurt, West Germany. The trans-Atlantic flight gave me time to relax and rest, but I felt

I was getting farther away from Muffin and Elizabeth because my memories of them were mostly in Florida. In Austria there would also be memories of Muffin and Elizabeth because we visited there in June before the wreck in July. My emotions were in turmoil. Although I knew from the encounter with the angel and also because of Muffin's faith that they were in Heaven, I continued to miss them. There was still the pain of separation and the depression of loneliness. They made life fun. I also felt like an outcast, not part of a family, not fitting in anywhere.

I was venturing into the world again as I had done many times before, but this time I had no real home ready for my return. My father died at age eighty-five, and my mother Roselle's health was failing. I needed to find a new life for myself. I struggled with my thoughts and emotions and finally went to sleep. I woke up early in the morning in Frankfurt because of the six-hour time difference. I was pleased the flight was smooth and problem free. I got on a local flight to Linz, Austria where my relatives would meet me. This flight was also smooth until we approached Linz and were denied permission to land because of heavy fog.

The airplane was circling Linz and flew near the Czech frontier as it continued to circle. I looked out the window and surprisingly saw no fog on the Czech side of the boundary. The ground was higher there and rose into some mountains just inside Czechoslovakia. Then I saw something startling. Below us in plain view, the East Bloc tanks were starkly massed all along the border. They were menacingly lined up side by side in a frontal formation facing downhill, guns pointed toward Austria, making a silent statement with thunderous significance. Some of the defense issues the angel discussed with me were suddenly showing up. Did God bring me to Austria to open my eyes to some of the real world defense situations involved in my assignments from the angel?

I was jolted into an analysis of the threat as the jet seemed to circle endlessly. I decided to find out more while I was in Austria. The neutrality of Austria was guaranteed by a treaty with France, Great Britain, the United States, and the Soviet Union. Austria had a very small self-defense force of approximately 58,000. East Bloc tanks should not be poised to launch a major offensive into Austria unless there was a plan to attack Western Europe through neutral Austria as the path of least resistance and as a quick way to separate some of the Southern Western Allies from the others. Italy, Yugoslavia, Greece, and Turkey could be cut off, and Austria could be used as a base for further East Bloc offensives into Western and Northern Europe.

As I thought about the serious situation, the flight was finally diverted to Vienna. I would not be going to Linz as planned. Upon landing in Vienna, we were told a bus would take us back from Vienna to Linz, but there was also heavy fog on the Autobahn. After fitful stops and starts creeping along in the fog, the bus arrived in Linz six hours later in the middle of the night. I received a message at the Vienna Airport to go to the train station in Linz, but the bus driver was not allowed to take the bus to the train station, only to the bus station! I was put out in sub-freezing weather in front of the bus station with five huge pieces of luggage holding Christmas gifts from the family and a very large box containing a gift from me, a Weber charcoal grill.

There was no one to help me with my burden of baggage, but someone came out of the night and pointed down the street toward the train station "in that direction." I did not know how far. I could not see the train station, but I started moving my big pile in the designated direction. I moved the items one by one a short distance to make a new pile and kept repeating this relocation of the pile so my moving pile was slowly headed toward the train station, I hoped. The physical activity was helping me combat the biting cold weather with most of my warmer clothes still packed up in the suitcases of my gradually moving pile.

Then a passing car honked its horn at me, but I ignored it because I did not recognize the car. I was really in a vulnerable predicament standing in the street with my pyramid of baggage so late at night with no one around. To my surprise Audrey got out of the car, and Christian was in the driver's seat. I was being rescued! They borrowed a larger car because I had so much baggage. My prized pile on the edge of the street was quickly moved into the car. I settled swiftly into the warm car and asked, "How much farther was it to the train station?" They laughed and said, "You were right in front of the train station." I laughed too with relief. I was so intent on pushing my pile down the street I did not realize I was at the train station. The warmth in the car restored my circulation as I travelled with Audrey and Christian on the last segment of my very long journey to their village.

I was so tired I did not remember much after arriving at their house. The next morning, I woke up late. Then I was shown their parlor where I could relax, read my book, and work on my case that was scheduled in Milan after New Year's. The house was a big old three-story home passed down from the original village doctor to Christian's father to Christian. Most of the first floor was used for the medical clinic. The second floor was for family living along with part of the first floor including the kitchen, a small dining area, and the parlor. I read my book while the clinic was busy. Christian was working longer hours to get everyone healthy before the clinic closed for Christmas. Audrey showed me around the village during the warmest part of the day. With its small but very picturesque, beautiful village church, it was a storybook setting. I soon retreated to the warmth of their house where I spent most of my time reading my book, *On Wings of Eagles*. The weather improved after I arrived, so I could go outside to get some fresh air.

The book was about the rescue from Iran of some of Ross Perrot's employees after The Shah's rule was replaced in 1979 by a radical revolutionary regime. After The Shah left Iran to get cancer treatments, his Provisional Caretaker Government under Baktiar was overthrown.

Ross Perrot's Company, EDS (Electronic Data Systems), had a contract with the Shah's government to computerize the records of the Iranian Welfare Department. EDS shut down the manual system used to pay weekly benefits before the new system was working, causing delays in getting the payments out.

These weekly payments were used not only to assist the needy but as political payoffs to keep the Shah in power. The first week without "welfare" checks was a problem, and it got much worse each week until after six weeks, the government was overthrown in the rage caused by the lack of "welfare" payments.

Radical Iran arrested some of the EDS employees and demanded that a large bond be posted for their release. When they escaped with help from a rescue team sent by Ross Perrot, the Iranians took hostages at the U.S. Embassy to replace the EDS employees.

The seeds of future trouble were sown. The Shah's government may have eventually been overthrown because he left the country to get cancer treatments in the United States, but the collapse of the "welfare" payments system accelerated the downfall of westernized Iran. The United States Government was initially indecisive while the situation in Iran deteriorated, and the U.S. Embassy hostage crisis did not end until Ronald Reagan was inaugurated as President.

Reading this book and studying related events consumed most of my time for several days. I continued to study the Middle East closely after my work at the Navy headquarters in London the previous May where I reviewed all the reports and evidence from the suicide terrorist truck bombing of the U.S. Embassy in East Beirut, Lebanon in April, 1983. I was asked to initially assess responsibility and recommend measures to guard against future attacks. Now I wondered if my future work would deal more with terrorism or with the Soviet Union.

I studied Soviet foreign policy and Marxist political theory long ago at Emory and continued to watch developments in that area. Possibly I would be a peacemaker again as I was at the end of the Viet Nam War when my legal memo was used to break the deadlock in the truce negotiations in Paris in 1973. I thought I was almost finished with this type of work for the Navy before the wreck occurred five months earlier. After receiving information about the future from the angel, I was much more intense in pursuing these subjects now. As the angel said, when the time comes, I would know what I am supposed to do. I would not be taken by surprise.

CHAPTER 16
A HOWLING HOLIDAY BLIZZARD

I was thinking about my 42nd Birthday on December 22 when the weather suddenly turned bad, after the improved weather of the past week. It was soon obvious this storm was in a league by itself as a howling holiday blizzard hit us with full fury. Snow piled up in huge quantities. The strong winds and the severe wind chill were disabling, knocking you down and turning you into flash frozen flesh. The temperature was minus 15 degrees Fahrenheit or lower, so cold the heat indoors in the old house did not work. I slept in my clothes and my boots. I put on my overcoat and gloves before getting into my sleeping bag on top of a mattress on the floor in a room on the 3rd story of the old house. Now I was starting to think about survival. The Austrians were saying this was the worst blizzard in forty years (since December, 1944).

Suddenly the worst of the blizzard passed, leaving a winter wonderland of ice and snow. This was a White Christmas to equal or exceed any other White Christmas. The medical clinic was closed for Christmas, but Christian made a few last minute house calls to farms where the patients were unable to come into town. I went along on these house calls. Christian had a small car that would not get stuck in the snow and on the unpaved roads. The farms had an arrangement similar to Christian's clinic. The family's living quarters were in part of the building, and the cows were in another part of the building. This was a good arrangement in cold weather to feed and milk the cows and keep them alive during a blizzard.

On Christmas Eve, we went to the village church where they were singing Christmas songs. I could not translate the lyrics from German, but the music was absolutely beautiful. Then we returned to the clinic for a Christmas celebration. Tables were put together and covered to make a very large table. Crowding close together, everyone could sit at the same table. Christian's parents and his extended family came including the family of his brother. There was not much emphasis on gifts. The main focus was a family reunion and celebration of Christmas.

A real Christmas tree was brought in decorated with real candles burning with magnetic warmth, pulling us into the mood and emotional power of Christmas. Even as a complete novice in adorning Christmas trees with lighted candles, I was allowed to put around half of the candles on the tree and light them at the right time. Each candle had a little drip pan under it to catch the hot, dripping wax. The fire hazard I feared was under control, and the candles were blown out at the end of the family gathering to symbolize the end of the evening.

After Christmas, Christian and Audrey, who was the clinic's manager, had several days off from work and offered to show me some of Austria while taking me to Vienna. I was leaving my comfortable Christmas cocoon in the storybook village. One morning we got into their car and headed toward Vienna, but we soon detoured without explanation. We seemed to be lost and getting more lost. We were driving around in a neighborhood of a town near Linz. Christian finally stopped and said, "I think this is it, but let me make sure." He jumped out of the car and went to the front door of a house. A man opened the door, and Christian motioned for us to get out of the car and come to the house. We must really be lost if he needs so much help with directions that we need to come inside while he gets his questions answered about how to find our way back onto the route to Vienna.

When I walked into the house, Christian introduced me to his cousin, his cousin's wife, their children, and guests as everyone laughed at my surprise. It was a perfect surprise. I never suspected anything. These were some of Christian's relatives who could not come to the Christmas Eve dinner at the clinic, so they invited us to have lunch with them after Christmas. It was a minor detour on the way to Vienna, and they were having fun meeting and teasing an American. Christian's cousin had two beautiful blond daughters who giggled and flirted with me.

So we could reach Vienna that evening, they quickly invited us to sit down around a small table and have lunch. A small sofa was pulled up on one side of the table, and I was told to sit there. One of the attractive young ladies sat down beside me and told me to move toward the center of the sofa. Then the slightly older blond beauty sat down on the other side of me, pinning me between the two sisters. Everyone thought my blushing was very funny. When everyone was seated, the food was brought out including a small silver serving dish with a silver cover that came last with a flourish. It was announced as a special food to honor their American guest. It was passed to me first, and I said, "Thank you." When I removed the silver dish cover, it was catsup. They laughed loudly at my complete surprise, and the host said, "Americans put catsup on everything, so we save this catsup for our American friends. We do not use it."

I put a small amount of catsup on my plate and thanked them for paying special attention to me. I said, "Your food is so good I don't need any catsup, but if this were American food, I would need to put some catsup on it." They were pleased with my compliment, and Christian's cousin said, "If you don't want any catsup, we will put it away and enjoy our lunch. We will save the catsup for other Americans."

The enjoyable lunch with the great home-cooked food ended all too soon. We separated after lunch into ladies' and men's groups for conversation and visiting. Two of the men guests were engineers with the power company. They talked about power sharing on the electricity grid between Eastern and Western Europe. Some of the cooperating engineers on the Eastern side told them if there were hostilities with the West (NATO), the Eastern Bloc planned to overload the Western grid, sending massive amounts of electricity from the East. This would shut down everything in the West and allow Warsaw Pact forces to advance in the chaos.

They were concerned about the numerical superiority of the Warsaw Pact forces until they realized each of our fifty states has a National Guard in addition to our national army. We had units of our national army deployed in defensive positions along the "Iron Curtain" dividing Europe during the cold war. They said, "Well, if you have fifty armies in addition to your national army, we won't worry. You can reinforce. You don't need to keep such a large army here as the Warsaw Pact does."

Our holiday visit ended quickly. We said our goodbyes and resumed our journey to Vienna. I knew I would probably never see them again. The two sisters cheered me up and reminded me I was alive with a future that could be normal. The slightly older young lady spoke English better than her younger sister, and she had a stronger attraction because of her lively, engaging personality. They were both exquisite, but neither one was the girl I saw during my encounter with the angel. They made a special effort to be kind to me and enable me to have some fun. My moping was delightfully disrupted, and my overall mood was more cheerful as we continued on our way to Vienna.

We reached the Autobahn at Linz, but it was partially closed because there was so much snow. It was travel at your own risk. The huge snow plows were busy working to clear the road. Christian had snow tires, so we went ahead very slowly. Visibility was poor, but I helped watch the road, nervously sitting in the front passenger seat. We made some progress toward Vienna, and the snow diminished until the road and the weather were basically clear but extremely cold. I thought about how God apparently had several reasons for bringing me to Austria. In addition to my work and my personal recovery, I was confronted with the harsh front-line realities of the Cold War. I was apparently being prepared for more involvement in national defense as I moved along toward Vienna on my personal road to recovery and toward my resumption of international work that was waiting for me.

We passed some spectacular castles on the Autobahn, and then we reached Vienna. Christian had another cousin with an apartment in Vienna. We were able to stay in that apartment as the owner was away for the holidays. I was shown the city with its grandeur and beauty. We visited the Vienna Woods (Wienerwald) hill park on the edge of the city. There were many cars painted unusual shades of blue and green. Christian explained these colors were "Kaiser blue" and "Kaiser green," two of the former Emperor's favorite colors that remained popular long after the monarchy ended in 1919 following the First World War.

As we drove around so I could see the city from inside the warmth of the car, we crossed the bridge over the Danube River toward "U.N. City" where the United Nations has headquarters for some of its organizations. I looked down at the river below, and it looked like ice. I asked if the Danube ever froze over at Vienna. Christian said, "The last time it froze over at Vienna was forty years ago in December, 1944, and I don't think it's freezing over now." I asked him if the other rivers in Eastern Europe froze over solid in December, 1944, and he said, "Yes." I realized this changed history. The Red Army advancing from the East did not need bridges. They crossed the rivers on solid ice while the armies of the Western Allies waited for a bridge over the Rhine. This placed the Red Army in control of Eastern Europe and allowed the Red Army to reach Berlin for the final battle ahead of the Western Allies. When we crossed back over the Danube, Christian looked down at the ice below and said, "The river is freezing over solid now."

The next day we continued sightseeing around the city. We toured one of the former royal palaces where I heard the story of the origin of the crescent roll. The bakers who got up to work long before sunrise heard the sounds of the Turks tunneling under the walls and gave the alarm, saving the city that was under siege by the Ottomans. The Emperor decreed that the bakers should make a special bread to celebrate the victory over the Turks, and the crescent roll was made in the shape of the crescent moon on the Turkish flag. That evening we went to a holiday concert at one of the symphonies for which Vienna is famous.

On New Year's Eve, it was time for Christian and Audrey to return home, and I checked into a second floor room of a hotel on the main plaza in the center of old Vienna to spend the night. From my window, I faced the old cathedral in the plaza. I was staying in the hotel so I could get a taxi very early the next morning to the Vienna Airport for my 8 a.m. flight departure to Milan. I made arrangements in advance for a taxi as it was a holiday, and I could not afford to miss my flight. I learned the cathedral was St. Stephen's and that the plaza was St. Stephen's Plaza. I was offered a tour of the catacombs under the old church, but I was not interested in more contact with death. Even though it was part of history, it was too personal for me.

I also learned that St. Stephen's Plaza (Stefansplatz) is the equivalent of Times Square where the people traditionally celebrate the New Year with champagne, but not French champagne. Austria makes plenty of its own as a major grape producer in Europe. I realized something really big was about to happen. The plaza started to fill up with people until it was totally packed with very cramped standing room only. I was alone and had an important early morning flight. I decided to watch from my hotel window, a ringside seat in the middle of everything. As the celebration escalated in numbers and noise, I needed to get some sleep. My accumulated fatigue was catching up with me. I fell asleep to what sounded like many automatic weapons firing, but it was actually the sound of thousands of champagne corks popping out of the bottles. Many of the corks even bounced and rattled off my window, but I slept anyway, anticipating the next morning after it was all over.

CHAPTER 17
HIJACKED

At 6 a.m. the next morning, I walked across the plaza with my luggage (much lighter now) to the taxi waiting for me with the motor running. The taxi could not get any closer to the hotel because of the frozen glaze of empty champagne bottles from the night before, littering the plaza. No one else was out except us. The plaza was now eerily silent and empty. I felt better inside the heated taxi headed for the airport, but I was concerned about the time. The driver passed close to the Hungarian border and brought me to the airport at 6:30 a.m. I was surprised I was on time and went to check in.

It was snowing, and the airport was going to close because of heavy snow on the runways with more bad weather on the way. Passengers could check in but without any guarantee the flight would be able to take off. I did not want to check in for this flight, but there was no alternative. Then the airline agent said the flight was oversold because it was the only flight that might go that day. He told me I would be upgraded to first class or bumped off the flight if I refused to be upgraded.

I did not want to be upgraded to first class. In foreign travel I tried to avoid first class so as not to call attention to myself as an American alone in the world. I checked in anyway because I had to get to Milan on schedule. The flight was delayed as I waited wearily with the other passengers. The airport maintenance crews finally rolled out huge metal mesh mats on one of the runways that were like gigantic metal mesh doormats. This was done to provide traction for the jet's tires. Then we boarded the plane. If the jet was unable to take off, we would come back to the terminal.

The jet was pushed to the runway and placed in position to race its engines for takeoff. The jet was fully loaded and possibly overloaded. The brakes were released, and the jet started down the runway making a strange scraping, grating noise on the metal mesh mats. The airplane looked like a big drag racer, spinning its wheels and throwing geysers of ice and snow behind it. We were not going nearly fast enough for takeoff as the jet lumbered and thrashed its way down the runway through the ice and snow. Then we ran out of metal mesh matting as the plane shuddered, and the takeoff was about to be aborted in a very messy way. At that moment the huge jet finally lifted slightly into the air and seemed about to settle back down on the ground. We were flying very low and slow just above the runway until we began to slowly climb and gain altitude. There was spontaneous applause from the passengers for the pilot's performance. He announced we were the first and last flight out that day. The airport was being closed behind us. No more takeoffs would be attempted until conditions improved.

We climbed for a long time to gain enough altitude to get over the nearby Alps to reach sunny Italy on the other side. I thought about how I was under a doctor's care for the past two weeks with Christian watching over me, making sure I got enough rest and study time along with positive activities and exercise to help me recover. He also made me feel I was helpful to him and others, that I had worth and was not finished. Although he was a relative, he approached my situation with expertise gained from his medical experience. Now I was on my own again, alone. Then as the flight finally began to level off for cruising, there was a disturbance in First Class.

One of the passengers two rows forward and across the aisle from me stood up and started screaming and yelling as he made threatening gestures. My worst fears were being realized while I was a sitting duck in First Class. I put my head down and thought this must be a diversion so the hijackers could make their move while everyone was distracted by this disturbance. I would be a prized hostage as an American and a Navy Officer sitting in

First Class. The man kept yelling and screaming, but nothing happened. Why were they waiting so long to make their move?

Everyone was in shock and paralyzed by fear. Then the unruly passenger's seatmate on the aisle side returned from the restroom and pushed him back into his seat by the window. The seatmate quieted his riotous companion. Everyone was relieved but still uneasy as to whether or not the incident was over. It turned out to be a false alarm caused by a mental patient from a wealthy Austrian family. His companion caretaker was taking his patient to Italy for the rest of the winter. When our flight landed in Milan, we were taken off the airplane and taken to the terminal. Everyone kept completely away from these two men, fearing that the situation might not be over. I was thankful for God's mercy extended to me again. I remembered some of my other close calls before the wreck including the crash landings of two commercial airliners where I walked away uninjured both times. I was especially grateful for God's faithful protection over and over through the years.

After this false alarm thoroughly rattled my nerves, I was glad to go to the Hilton Hotel and check in safely. In my room the metal roll down shutters were completely closed over the sliding glass door to the outside balcony. This must have been overlooked by housekeeping, so I raised the shutters. Soon I was contacted by hotel management who told me to put the shutters down again. I was told there had been some attacks by Red Brigade terrorists, so I put the shutters down. I left a small space at the bottom that I hoped could not be seen from outside because of the safety wall enclosure around the bottom of the balcony.

After sleeping uneasily, I woke up the next morning ready to take care of the long awaited business on the tuna fish claim. I contacted the client's representative, Gary, from San Diego who was meeting me in Milan. We went to lunch with the boss of the company that purchased the frozen tuna fish for a cannery in Italy. I had the locally relished black pasta and was accepted as a visitor who appreciated Italian food. My appreciation was genuine.

That afternoon we worked late into the evening to complete all of the witness statements, leaving the following day open if anything was overlooked. The next day when everything appeared to be completed satisfactorily, we went shopping for gifts to take home. Instead of my usual shopping for Muffin and Elizabeth, I went with Gary to help him buy a suede jacket for his wife. Gary did not like to negotiate prices with vendors, and he was an important client. I learned this bargaining practice early when I was a young teenager visiting Mexico. I enjoyed the give and take interaction with the sellers.

Milan is the fashion capital of Italy, and we went to the Courso de Buenos Aires where the retail center of the fashion district is located. At the end of World War II, Argentina gave a tremendous amount of assistance to war-torn Northern Italy, and the main street in the fashion district was named after the Argentine capital. We were shopping in the shadow of history, and we needed to quickly acquire the right gifts to bring home for family members. We had no time for sightseeing.

We looked in a very expensive store. While I went along with Gary, I decided to buy a similar jacket for Muffin's Aunt Carole. She and her husband Uncle Don Elliott had always done so much for us. The jacket we wanted was $4,400.00, not Lira but Dollars! We could not pay that much nor would we if we could! We heard these jackets were expensive, and this seemed to prove what we heard. Next, we wandered into a more average store next door that had all types of merchandise. They had several of the types of jackets we wanted for over $200.00 but not in the right sizes. They asked if we could wait while they got the correct sizes for us. We waited a few minutes, and they came back with two jackets. Both were the exact sizes we needed, and both jackets looked like the same jackets we had seen in the expensive store next door.

I wondered if when they went out the back door of their store to get the correct sizes if they had gone in the back door of the store next door to get the same jackets we had already shopped. Later when we went back to the store next door, the jackets were gone. Now the right jackets were in front of us for $219.00. Gary was ready to pay and go, but I asked him if I could negotiate. I told the sales person the jackets were overpriced and had been handled by too many people. The price was gradually negotiated down in stages to $159.00. Gary was very happy and said, "You saved me $60.00." I was thinking it was a much bigger savings because we started next door at $4,400.00, but clients often undervalue the work of their lawyers, so I just nodded my agreement.

I asked for the same price on the other jacket I was getting for Aunt Carole, but the sales clerk said, "Oh, no, I did you a favor by reducing the price for your friend. I could see that was very important to you. Now you have to do me a favor and pay the full price for the other jacket." The clerk was insistent I had to repay the favor and finally came down only $10.00 for me. I had to have the jacket. They were hard to find, and time was running out, so I paid $209. I kept telling myself it was a very good price compared to what it would cost back home in the States or in the better stores in Milan. As our shopping was rushed to completion, I bought a silk necktie for myself and a red little girl's overcoat for Jennifer, the daughter of my cousin John who came to the hospital in the middle of the night so I could be treated for my injuries.

With our business and shopping finished, Gary and I said goodbye that afternoon as he got out of the taxi. We would be on different flights back to San Diego and Miami. Although I represented Gary in another case later with his own company, I was sorry I never saw him again after Milan. Working with him in Milan was a positive experience for me, helping relieve my gloomy personal attitude. The next day, I went to the Milan Airport. While I was waiting for departure, the bomb sniffing dogs passed. A hush fell over the entire room until the dogs passed by without alerting. Talking resumed nervously. The use of bomb sniffing dogs in the airport showed me terrorism in the area was a real threat. I was glad when it was time to enter the secured area for flight departure. There was already enough risk and difficulty for one trip.

I don't remember much about the return flights. I slept a lot. As I departed Milan, I remember thinking about everything that happened, "What is next? Will we ever find the prior records of the defendant?" Then I thought about what happened in Milan. The angel was right again! It would not have happened without me. No one else would have taken so much time and gone to so much trouble to be in Milan at the right time to take the statements. Many lawyers would not have gotten security for the claim outside the United States. They would have told their clients to write off the large loss as unrecoverable, that the ship was outside our jurisdiction and beyond the reach of our legal process.

So, I returned home in one piece needing to catch up on other claims and take care of other business. The trip was very worthwhile and was a turning point in getting me back on track. God had orchestrated a symphony of support for me wherever I went. Upon returning home, I was making plans to pass my annual Navy medical physical exam in early February, 1985, but I was still angry that my good wife and family and my good life were hijacked and destroyed by a drunken, drugged criminal who had no real remorse and who was in the process of trying to get away with it one more time. But God had other plans.

CHAPTER 18
DAY OF RECKONING

It was late in the afternoon the day before the 9 a.m. February court date in the criminal case, and there were still no prior criminal records of the defendant. At the very last possible moment as I was agonizingly praying about the situation and asking God why no records had been found as the angel said, I received a telephone call from New York asking the name and FedEx delivery address of the prosecuting attorney handling the criminal case for the State of Florida. I was informed the defendant's prior criminal records in Connecticut and New York had been located and were being sent overnight to Miami for delivery at 8 a.m. the next morning, just one hour before the scheduled court appearance. I was electrified by this almost past the last minute development that only God could arrange with such breathtaking minutely calibrated timing. But I was not really surprised after all. As they say in baseball, the angel was still batting a thousand.

There was a last minute delay in the court proceedings early the next morning as the attorneys reviewed and evaluated this new information they were seeing for the first time. This surprise development occurring "on the courthouse steps" on the way to the hearing crushed the defendant's strategy. He was successfully portraying himself as a first offender, but between 8 a.m. and 9 a.m., he finally faced reality. Instead of the fictitious self-portrait of himself he had been painting for months, he was now completely exposed in his true light. After a further short delay, the defendant abruptly changed his plea to guilty. Then the Judge questioned him about his plea, if he understood what he was doing and if his plea was freely and voluntarily entered. After questioning the defendant fully, the Judge accepted his guilty plea and scheduled a sentencing hearing later in February to allow time for completion of a pre-sentencing report from the probation officers, including the defendant's very recently revealed prior criminal record. The defendant decided pleading guilty and asking the court for leniency was in his best interests now that his previous record was known.

The preparation for the sentencing hearing was very intense as Florida law allows statements for the record from victims of crimes. Muffin's mother spoke first, talking about the wonderful individuals the defendant callously snuffed out and pointing out the defendant never expressed remorse or apologized to any family members. He never asked to be forgiven. He spoke to the Judge about leniency but not to the family. When the defendant said he was sorry, he only addressed the Judge and not the family.

When I spoke, I was asking for a sentence to fit the crimes, not a short sentence! I introduced the mortality tables that were part of Florida law so the Judge could consider them. I pointed out the defendant not only killed Muffin and Elizabeth, but he also robbed them of combined life expectancies totaling 127 years. Even the maximum sentence would be nowhere close to 127 years. The Judge acted within the Florida sentencing guidelines, requiring the defendant to serve two sentences of five years each (one for each death) to be served consecutively for a total of ten years and revoked the defendant's driver's license for twenty years.

The total of ten years in prison was fair. It could not be reversed on appeal because it was neither excessive nor lenient under the sentencing guidelines. Revoking his driver's license for twenty years, while apparently tough, could have the effect of sending the Defendant to yet another state when he was released from prison after serving less than seven years with the benefit of good time and gain time while in prison. He could do the same thing again. He could apply for a driver's license in another state, indicating he had no prior offenses. He probably would not stay in Florida for another thirteen years without a driver's license. He could surface in another state, posing as a first offender if he got in trouble there.

This is similar to what happened in Connecticut and New York when his prior criminal records were concealed. Charges were pending against the defendant in a small New York town, and the prosecuting attorney apparently held the charges and the prior criminal records on his desk if the defendant would get out of town and stay out. If he showed up in town again, the charges would be pressed including reference to his prior offenses. The charges and prior record apparently stayed on a prosecuting attorney's desk in New York for an extended period of time outside of the usual records system until an inquiry was made by a resident of that district. Then the prior records were suddenly disclosed and on their way to Florida for an early morning delivery just before the scheduled court hearing.

I thanked God the criminal case was now over. Just as life itself, it was not perfect, but the defendant was held accountable. He did not get away with his crimes. I was very grateful for the efforts of all who were involved as witnesses, in obtaining evidence and in arresting, testing, and prosecuting him. When the criminal case was finally over, I counted eleven times I had been to Court including witness statements, transcript corrections at the Court Reporter's Office, and sentencing. Although the case took a long time, it was concluded much sooner than most criminal cases as we learned from others. Muffin and Elizabeth could not be brought back, but the defendant had been brought to justice. While he evaded human justice before, it was different when God weighed in as stated by the angel in the encounter.

The angel had been right about the details, too. If I had not lived and met with my Navy friends in New York at the Europa Café, the defendant's prior record would not have been known. I would not have looked so long for his prior record if the angel had not told me about it along with God's intention to bring the defendant to justice now. I would not have been a witness, and I would not have been able to help with the statements for the victims at sentencing. The rearview mirror eyewitness in the other pickup truck going away from the wreck would also not have been discovered if I died, another reason the angel gave me why I must live. There would have been no Steve Tarr representing me and no investigator working for Steve to track down witnesses. The angel was accurate far beyond human knowledge and abilities, but what about the rest of what the angel said that had not happened yet?

PART II

RESUMING LIFE

After the defendant changed his plea to guilty and was sentenced in February, 1985, I was free to focus on the future and resume a more normal life apart from continually re-living the fatal wreck, its terrible tragedies, and its immediate aftermath. My faith in what the angel told me was getting stronger as major unfolding events continued to provide more and more proof.

CHAPTER 19
PURSUING THE PATH TO RECOVERY

At the sentencing hearing, I still showed signs of physical and mental suffering although there was progress in some areas of recovery. I was photographed by news media leaving the Courtroom. I looked terrible and was having trouble walking and carrying my briefcase and papers. I looked much older than my actual age of forty-two. All of my life I looked younger than my actual age. Most people guessed around ten years younger than my real age. This was an issue for me when appearing in Court.

Judges would sometimes jokingly ask me if I was old enough to be a lawyer, but it was a cutting query cloaked in humor to safely make fun of me! I was also sometimes addressed by Judges as "whipper snapper" and asked if I had taken the bar exam yet. These are examples of what I faced, but it was outweighed by the advantages of looking younger. The opposition would often underestimate me and be surprised when I was ready with a well prepared presentation.

My hair turned back to its normal darker color. As I left the courtroom when the sentencing was over, I knew a major chapter in my life was closing in spite of my continuing emotional and physical difficulties resulting from the wreck. Closing the criminal case also brought the insurance claims to the brink of settlement as the other driver's responsibility was now established. The insurance claims were very close to settlement in the following month of March, 1985. Steve Tarr was surprised when I insisted on a structured settlement paying me monthly instead of grabbing as much cash as possible immediately. I remembered what the angel said in the encounter. I would need sustaining resources over time to survive and do the jobs outlined for me in the encounter. So I asked in my vulnerable situation to protect the settlement money by having it paid in long-term monthly payments.

However, the insurance company was not quite ready to settle. I was sent to a psychiatrist for evaluation. I am not sure why because he was not able to find anything wrong with me mentally. He kept suggesting I should be angry with Muffin and Elizabeth as this is normal when close family members die. Although he was a very caring doctor, I thought he was nuts. I was a victim of violent crime. I was injured by the same defendant who killed Muffin and Elizabeth and thought he killed me. I had a bond with them even after they died. We suffered together and died together. I was angry with the defendant, not with his other victims. I was one of his victims! I could understand what the psychiatrist was saying if their deaths were natural deaths, possibly caused by some neglect or lack of care by them, but there was no reason to be angry with them or to blame them. They were blameless! After several sessions, I quit going to him, but I was determined to be sane by an expert.

After I stopped going to the psychiatrist, the insurance claims were settled with a structured settlement in March, 1985 with the first monthly payment in April, 1985. Now the aftermath of the wreck was being resolved so I could focus more on the path to recovery, what might be in the future for me and less on the immediate past with its terrible tragedies, losses, and lingering disabilities.

During this time, my mother Roselle was concerned that I still needed more medical help. She found out Dr. Walter Jones was an orthopedic doctor in Coral Gables. He was from the same hometown of Cairo, Georgia where I was born and where his father had been a respected pastor. So I went to see Dr. Walter Jones. He was actually the team physician for the Miami Dolphins. He was very good and took some x-rays. He was also very honest. He told me there was not much if anything that could be done for me that had not already been done. I would gradually get worse over time as I aged. I asked him if there was anything that might help. He thought and then said, "Exercise might help." When I asked him, "How much exercise?" He said, "I don't know, it's an individual thing; it varies." I decided to find out how much exercise might help me in my situation.

I asked Dr. Jones what type of exercises would be good. He said whatever exercises I could do with my injuries. I specifically asked him if I could do pushups, and he said, "No, you might re-fracture your right elbow because it was fractured right at the tip, and pushups would put tremendous stress on your elbow." Then I asked him about sit ups, thinking that might help with the injuries in my lower back and pelvic areas. He said, "No, that could injure you more because of the serious conditions you have in those areas." I thanked him for his evaluation and advice, but I never went back to him again after the initial visits. He made it clear I was on my own now to deal with my situation on a trial and error basis with exercises, going as far as I could each time without hurting myself. That was the beginning of an intense, prolonged exercise program lasting over three years.

My exercise was usually in the mornings, consisting of running in place on a small personal trampoline along with some other moderate exercises and stretches. I typically exercised every other day. Then I would take a hot shower to clean up and help with the muscle spasms and other soft tissue injuries. The upper part of my right leg was still mangled where the metal ribs of the small folding umbrella were driven into my leg by the impact of the collision. Working with my injuries by exercising regularly was gradually helping me, but it was also a constant reminder of the wreck and its tragedies. I was able to spend more time in the office working, and I resolved to work harder in my business to catch up after missing so much time from work

In the shower each time, I experienced another persistent problem. The hot water opened my pores, and fragments of glass worked their way to the surface of my forehead and the front area of hair on my head. These fragments of glass were numerous and would fall to the floor of the shower. I was horrified by this situation, but I left this process alone and let it work itself out on its own. I remembered what the plastic surgeon said how digging around and messing with the small imbedded fragments under my skin would do more harm than good. I was careful not to step on these sharp glass fragments in the shower with my bare feet. Some of these glass fragments were easily visible. Over many months the emerging glass fragments gradually became smaller and less numerous, although there are still sometimes small particles like very gritty grains of sand coming out over twenty-seven years later.

I was doing well enough after the sentencing hearing that I passed my annual Navy Reserve Physical Exam later in February, 1985. The doctor said I had low blood pressure and a low pulse rate of a healthy teenager. When I had eighteen previous annual physicals plus my original induction physicals, I was never told that my blood pressure and pulse rate were typical of a much younger person. In my thirteen annual physicals that followed up until my last annual physical in 1998, I continued to hear similar comments from the doctors. As I became older in actual age, they were more amazed and would ask me how I did it. I usually mentioned diet, exercise, and the avoidance of habits harmful to health, but I wondered about when the angel healed me. Did he re-set my body clocks so I was aging from the date of the wreck?

CHAPTER 20
TAKING THE INITIATIVE

With the first monthly settlement check, it was time to look ahead. I wanted to take the initiative rather than respond to emerging events. I planned to go to London in early May to work on some cases and to meet with my claims clients at Lloyd's of London and other contacts in London. I had already been back to New York following the wreck, and I wanted to dispel any misconceptions in London about my ability to continue working effectively for them. I wanted to convince them I was more committed and determined than ever to get great results for them.

I was also preparing for the annual Navy physical fitness test in July. It would be more difficult for me to pass than the annual medical physical exam in February. In July I would be required to do some pushups, sit ups, and run a mile and a half within a required time. I focused on this throughout April and planned to work on it while in London. In spite of the conservative advice from Dr. Walter Jones, I decided to do some sit ups and pushups to stay in the Navy. Although the national defense situation was temporarily quiet, I needed to be ready, and I needed to be in the Navy. In Austria, God had given me an eyewitness view of the military realities and risks in Europe. I received special insight into potential conflicts and tactics there including the possible effect of severe weather.

The sit ups were very painful, and I could only do a few at first. However, I was in a weight lifting physical education class in college at Emory where I worked my way up to 152 sit ups at one time. Now I improved rapidly in the number of sit ups. As I increased the number of sit ups, the pain lessened so I sought to do more and more sit ups to diminish the pain. Pushups were different. They were always my weak area. With my injured elbow, I could not even do one push up. My injured right arm would not support my weight for a single push up. I was totally frustrated and very angry. I thought this would terminate my Navy career.

I decided to do a push up or break my arm trying. If my arm was broken, it could possibly be reset better than the way it healed after the wreck. I tried agonizingly for several days and finally did one push up with a loud yell! This achievement spurred me to intensify my efforts. I began to believe I could improve enough to pass the test in July. I became a fanatic, exercising ferociously every other day, trying to do a little more each time. By early May when it was time to go to London, I was struggling intensely to do three pushups.

The relative calm of preparing to resume my work in London was suddenly interrupted on Monday May 6, 1985 by an unexpected telephone call from Navy headquarters in Norfolk. A Captain I did not know was on the phone. He said, "Commander Bell, I am calling to give you a 'heads up' so you will not be surprised. You will be receiving a letter notifying you of a staff meeting in Norfolk on May 18 you will be expected to attend. You will be the legal officer for an operational exercise planned for September involving The Straits of Florida and how to keep the straits open for shipping in the event of hostilities. Is there any reason you cannot accept this assignment?" I remembered the angel said I would not be surprised, and I would "know what to do when the time comes."

This situation seemed to fit what the angel said. The Captain gave me a courtesy call so I would not be surprised, and I had local knowledge about The Straits of Florida. I also had detailed technical data about the structure and configuration of the straits and its Florida Reef. I confirmed I would be available for the assignment, and the Captain provided more details. I told him I would be in London soon and would do some research while there to help with the exercise based upon what he was telling me. Everything was agreed, and the call ended. I was thinking, if he had called a day later, he would have missed me. I would not have known to do anything while I was in London. God had arranged perfect timing while again verifying the veracity of my encounter with the angel. In August, 1976, while I was at the Naval War College, I helped plan for similar situations to keep the Straits of Hormuz open to shipping in and out of the Persian Gulf. This confirmed I was called correctly for this new assignment.

The flight from Miami to London on Tuesday, May 7 was long but smooth except for the usual turbulence over the mostly sunken mid-Atlantic ridge where possibly the lost continent of Atlantis was located. Part of the ridge was above water in the Azores and the Canary Islands and farther north in Iceland. I thought about this mystery until the turbulence subsided, and then my thoughts turned to the new day dawning in England where I would soon be arriving at Heathrow Airport on Wednesday morning, May 8. I would go through passport control, collect my baggage, clear customs, and take a taxi to the Savoy Hotel. I always wanted to stay there, and now it was possible through a discount offered with the annual maritime industry formal dinner held at the Savoy Hotel. I was scheduled to attend the reception and dinner there Thursday evening.

Later, when I arrived at the Savoy Hotel, I noticed something bigger than my annual maritime industry dinner was scheduled. The next day, Thursday, May 9 would be the 40th Anniversary Celebration of Victory in Europe in World War II. This V-E Day would be especially important because most veterans would still be participating, but by the time of the 50th Anniversary, many veterans would be gone or in poor health and much older. This celebration on May 9, 1985 would feature a tremendous amount of still living history, and as an amateur historian, I was delighted at the timing of my business trip to London. After checking into the Hotel around noon Wednesday and settling in my room, I called my cousin to let him know I was in town again. Patrick was my mother's first cousin. He was an American veteran who married Joyce, an English girl, when they were both working in New York City. After they returned to England, he worked for the Financial Times and encouraged me in my work with Lloyd's of London and other English clients.

Next, I called my contacts to schedule meetings, work on claims, and get instructions on claims from my clients. I was getting very busy, and then I remembered the Navy assignment to research the Straits of Florida situation. I decided to look in the law book stores for anything recently published that was helpful. I needed to look in the law book stores for books to update my civilian law library. I knew there were very helpful legal reference books in England that were not available in the United States.

I was not familiar with the first book shop where I stopped. It was not one where I shopped before. It was a regular book shop that apparently did not focus on law books. I was not familiar with the area where it was located. I was just walking toward the Chancery Lane area where several law book stores were located when I noticed a bookstore I had not seen before. I was in a hurry, but I went into the store anyway because I was curious to look inside a different bookstore to see what was there. After I was inside looking around, I discovered the store had a very small section of law books in a back corner. I looked in that bookcase. There were some books on the lower shelves I could only see by getting down on the floor on my hands and knees.

On the bottom shelf, I suddenly found a book related to the situation in the Navy project. Standing by the bookcase with the book in my hands, I hurriedly started reading it. This was apparently exactly what I needed for the Navy project. It was very recently published in England but not yet for sale in bookstores in the United States. It was a valuable find! I paid for it with my own money without asking for reimbursement. It would also help me in my other work. I was amazed I had stumbled on this book in such a random unplanned manner. The dynamic, ongoing, interactive impact of my encounter with the angel apparently accurately affected astoundingly complex details.

As I left the bookstore, I was not surprised by these ongoing intricate developments in my life and missions. Although it continued to seem unreal to me, I was prepared by the encounter with the angel! I also remembered my college Bible class at Emory with Dean Rece. We studied a book about the Bible with the title, *The Book of the Acts of God*. It explained some of God's actions in ancient times. I could accept God's intriguing interaction in human events. I believe God is Holy Action personified, but I was amazed I was actually involved with God now in some of what He was doing. I thought this was something that happened to other people, something that I hear about or read about involving God and extraordinary individuals. The realization that an ordinary person like me was deeply involved and that my life was intertwined in some of what God was doing left me stunned every time another major detailed connection with the encounter showed up.

As I walked along, I realized I now had internationally recognized highly acceptable guidelines to help me use my technical data and other information for the Navy exercise. Armed with this recently published research and analysis, I would be able to help develop practical workable operational Rules of Engagement (ROE) based on the highest standards of current international law. I would be able to help plan for the successful deployment and engagement of Navy forces to protect shipping and Navy convoys in the Straits of Florida. I continued looking in other bookstores, but no one else had the recently published book I found while hurriedly straying from my usual path.

I was excited and exhilarated by the sudden, unexpected momentum created by this unusual discovery. I felt this was the start of a surge of success, moving inevitably forward toward a new Navy goal not reached before by me or the Navy. If an operational plan could be successfully developed that would virtually guarantee safe passage through the Straits of Florida for friendly shipping and Navy convoys, this would be a game changer affecting the outcome of conflicts elsewhere in the world, assuring resupply and reinforcement to reach our military and friendly forces. I felt this was a very big deal in the making like a train running down the track of destiny with God at the controls. I could not get over the fact I had no way of finding the right, recent reference by myself. I did not know the name of the author or the name of the book. I did not know where or when it was published. I did not know the name of the publisher or how the book was classified by subject matter. The book was so newly published this vital data was not available yet. The book was put right in front of me. It was placed in my random path so I stumbled on it. While it was impossible to find, it was made eerily impossible to miss, precisely when it was needed.

CHAPTER 21
FINISHING A WEEK IN LONDON

As I was watching the V-E Day observances on television on Thursday morning, May 9, I saw Prince Phillip with an inkling of humor read from the Book of Philippians. He said it was one of his favorite books in the Bible. Then I went to the maritime industry annual meeting that morning in the basement meeting room of the annex to the old Baltic Exchange Building (later blown up and destroyed by terrorists). After following up with contacts at the morning meeting, I attended the formal dinner that evening at the Savoy Hotel. As usual there were important contacts at the reception before the dinner and at the dinner where seating was assigned to facilitate making new contacts and renewing established contacts. The meal was a seven-course affair with considerable toasting to The Queen and the Royal Family, high ranking officials, and others. There was a humorous after-dinner speech at a level of serious comedy targeted at the audience and the maritime industry including the lawyers and marine insurance representatives. In the United States we would call this a roast, but I have never experienced anything equal to this "toast."

Friday morning, May 10, I visited the claims office at Lloyd's to work on claims and renew contacts, but they were very busy with other out-of-town visitors who were also there because of the maritime industry annual meeting and formal dinner. I would return Monday morning, May 13 for follow up. I was only able to take care of the most pressing business Friday morning and in very brief fashion, but I took notes on items to be covered Monday morning.

While in London I also needed to see Jeremy Thomas about the frozen tuna fish claim. It was always a pleasure to meet with

Jeremy Thomas (usually in the afternoon with tea) at his office near Lloyd's and across the street from the old Baltic Exchange Building. The Baltic Exchange is where vessels were chartered, and Jeremy's office was at the crossroads of the world's marine business and insurance. After Friday morning at the Lloyd's claims office and skipping lunch in the rush, it was time for me to go meet nearby with Jeremy Thomas Friday afternoon.

Jeremy was always very cordial and friendly. He thanked me for the witness statements I recently obtained in Milan, Italy and said he would be able to proceed with the claim in arbitration now. Jeremy was not stiff like some London lawyers. He was different and fun. When I went to his office in the afternoon to meet with him, everything was very proper. We conferred about the claim, and he called in his assistant to give her certain instructions about moving the claim forward in the London arbitration process. Then he had tea brought into his office for tea time, and we were served an afternoon cup of English tea. As our conference was concluding, he asked me to come with him. Then I was walking with him wherever he went while we talked at greater length, not only about the claim but about many different topics including family and personal news and activities. While it seemed we were wandering aimlessly at a very rapid pace, Jeremy knew where we were going. The next thing I knew, we stopped at a pub for more talk and refreshments. This was always a challenge for me to be friendly in a pub setting without drinking or drinking very little.

Soon, Jeremy was ready to go again as I almost ran to keep up with him. I have a very long stride and walk very fast, but keeping up with Jeremy was a challenge, somewhat like running through Central London and The West End with a galloping gazelle. His next stop was the train station for the line going to Strawberry Hill near his home. He insisted I come with him on the train. He said, "I will get you back to your hotel later." After completing the train ride, we stopped at a neighborhood pub. Jeremy introduced me to a high ranking official with Parliament. He said, "That's why we stopped here because I wanted you to meet my friend who works with Parliament." We had a great discussion about the political systems in England and the United States, and then Jeremy was ready to go again. We walked the short remaining distance to his house at a somewhat slower pace.

Jeremy's home was over 200 years old. At one time it belonged to Horace Walpole. Through the years it had been updated. When I first met Jeremy in November, 1977, he and his wife, Laila and their children lived in a very nice flat in London across the street from the Westminster Cathedral. He had owned his new home farther out from London for several years. As his family grew, a larger, different type of home was needed. It was very good to see Laila, Melissa, Christopher, and David again. Laila was also a lawyer, and her father was a well-known lawyer from India. Laila was not with a law firm in London like Jeremy, she had her own independent practice, and David, the youngest child, was less than two years old. Laila had a home office for her work similar to mine back in Florida, and I easily related to their entire family.

When I arrived, I thought I was being invited to dinner as on previous visits when Laila said, "Lovely to have you here again, Bob, and we are so sorry about your terrible tragedy and the loss of your family, but it is good to see you are doing well again." Then there was some more conversation catching up on recent activities and travels, but there was no movement toward dinner. I was beginning to think something was wrong, that my timing was not good, when Jeremy said, "Bob, I hope you don't mind, but I have two tickets for dinner across the street at St. George's College. There is a big dinner tonight, and I think you would enjoy it. St. George's is the evangelical order of the Catholic Church in England, and you are evangelical."

I felt strange when Jeremy told me to take both tickets as I was only one person, but I followed instructions as Jeremy always had something in mind. At the dinner I was soon seated at one of the tables where one of the priests was talking about having a personal relationship with Jesus Christ. I followed this discussion with great interest and agreed, commenting how God helps those who are part of His family as he helped me in my time of trouble and tragedy. I was beginning to tire when Jeremy showed up and joined the discussion. He was very lively as usual and soon asked for both of us to be excused as it was getting late. Then he realized it was too late for me to get a train back into London, and he said, "Bob, you will just have to stay the night with us." He showed me to a part of the house I had never seen before, and I was glad to rest and get some sleep. It had been a very long day Friday following the formal dinner at the Savoy the night before.

The next morning Jeremy said, "Let me show you around," and we got into his motor car with his youngest son David in his car seat. Jeremy showed me the areas near where he lived, and then said, "Let's go to Hampton Court," that was the country palace of Henry VIII. I was appreciative of this suggestion because of my interest in history, so I agreed and thanked Jeremy for his hospitality. He said, "It's not far from here," and we sped off in that direction with David observing everything. We did take a quick walk around Hampton Court, but Jeremy was in a hurry and was looking for something. It was the ice cream vendor that was our ultimate destination all along. Jeremy gave David two ice cream sandwiches. He made sure David enjoyed the ice cream by getting it all over his face and everything else. Jeremy was laughing at the comical ice cream mess and finally cleaned David up after he was finished.

By now it was afternoon and time for me to get back to London to contact my cousin Patrick about church the next day, and I said goodbye to everyone until my next trip to London. Jeremy put me back on a train to London, and I started looking forward to seeing my cousin and his family again. When I rang Patrick, he told me to meet him at Westminster Abbey in the morning for one of the Sunday services. He said his younger son Benjamin would be singing in the choir. Sunday afternoon I waited at the entrance as instructed by Patrick. When he arrived, he introduced me to one of the Deacons who brought us inside the choir enclosure where we were allowed to sit with the choir, and I saw Benjamin again. There was not much opportunity to visit as the choir was on cue to sing. The choir enclosure was situated so the members of the choir could not be seen by the audience while their singing would be heard throughout Westminster Abbey.

While there I learned there was continuous organized prayer in shifts around the clock from the time of King Edward the Confessor right up to the present time, praying for the monarch, the royal family and the nation, perhaps explaining the success of the kingdom and most of its rulers through the centuries. As soon as the service was over, Patrick and Benjamin had trains to catch, and we said goodbye until my next trip to London.

On Monday morning, I went to the claims office at Lloyd's to meet with my bosses, and I went to lunch with three of them. At lunch we talked business and discussed current issues. Then the conversation turned to spiritual matters, perhaps because I had suffered the loss of my family. One of my bosses brought up the subject by asking what was my understanding of being "born again." As I discussed my beliefs, each one gave his own views that were very similar to mine. I wondered why we never discussed this topic with my American clients, but it gave me an opportunity to witness to them and discuss part of the encounter. They were strengthened by my faith, and I was strengthened by theirs. The discussion comforted me and reassured me I had real friends at Lloyd's in the claims office.

Everything in London was finished all too soon, and Tuesday morning it was time to go to Heathrow for my return flight to Miami. As I departed, I was grateful everything was finished very positively. I knew I had to get home and go to Norfolk for the Project Staff Meeting on Saturday, May 18.

CHAPTER 22
MORE PAIN

On the flight back to Miami, I was thinking about my mother. She spent some time with me after the wreck, but she had to go home for a doctor's appointment. She found out she needed surgery for colon cancer. This was apparently completed successfully while I was getting back on my feet after the wreck. The surgeon said the operation was only a short-term fix. He could not say that the cancer had not spread.

My mother did not want chemo-therapy. It was marginally effective for colon cancer, and she did not want the side effects. She wanted to find out about alternatives. She let me take her to the Comprehensive Cancer Center at the University of Miami Medical School at Jackson Memorial Hospital. The doctor recommended vitamin therapy as it helps some patients. There seemed to be nothing to lose, and my mother liked the idea. It involved taking large doses of beta carotene vitamins. She started taking the vitamins immediately before she returned home from Miami. There was a very rapid improvement in her health and appearance.

When friends saw her, they thought it was a rumor about her having cancer because she looked so healthy. She was a flower enthusiast and had over 100 camellia plants in her yard. One was named for her that my father developed. They were both accredited flower show judges. My mother was a past president of the Garden Clubs of Georgia, a federation of garden clubs with over 23,000 members in a multitude of clubs across the state. She decorated the East Room (State Room) of The White House when Jimmy Carter became President, and she worked nationally to beautify the Interstate Highways and other roads.

She was on the National Board of the Garden Clubs of America when she became ill again.

In May, 1985, she returned to the hospital in Thomasville, Georgia for evaluation. The surgeon and his father before him were the family doctors for our surgeries for generations. I knew my mother would receive the best care, but I was making plans to be with her when she was admitted to the hospital during the week of May 20 following my Navy meeting in Norfolk on Saturday, May 18.

As soon as I got back from London on May 14, I was working on a fast turn-around to travel to Norfolk Friday afternoon, May 17. I was never in Norfolk before. I found my way in a hurry driving a rental car from the airport all over Norfolk until it was impossible to get lost. Saturday morning, I showed up early for the meeting, but it was in a different area of the Headquarters' complex. I walked a long time through the hallways of the connected buildings until I finally found the large meeting room upstairs in an annex building where the exercise was being planned. Most of the participants were there although the meeting had not officially started. The Admiral was not there yet, but the Executive Officer was checking off arrivals. He was surprised I was there because there were no paid orders for me as planned.

I explained I received a telephone call and a letter notifying me, so I came. He said they could still use my help if I was able to attend the monthly project staff meetings without pay. I remembered how I came to be there, and I agreed I would help without pay or travel reimbursements because of the importance of the project. The exercise leader was a commodore, but almost as soon as the meeting started, his boss who was a two-star Admiral came in to give us a pep talk and throw his support behind the exercise leader. As soon as the Admiral finished his opening remarks, one of the more senior captains asked two questions about the exercise bringing up issues that would be obstacles to the success of the exercise unless somebody could answer these two "show stopper" questions.

To the surprise of everyone, I raised my hand. I answered the two questions based upon the information I recently obtained in London. The Admiral looked somewhat surprised by my quick answers, but he looked at everyone else and said, "With this approach, I don't see any reason why the exercise cannot be successful. Guidelines can be included to handle these two issues." Then the Admiral got up, said goodbye and turned everything over to the Commodore. Everyone looked at me like they were wondering who I was, and where in the world did I come from? The meeting was a success, and I was able to get back to the airport on time for my flights to Tallahassee to see about my mother.

When I reached my mother's house, she had already left for the hospital. There was a message for me to come to the hospital the next morning, Monday, May 20. I met with the surgeon. He recommended a second operation but predicted it would not save my mother's life. The operation would reduce her pain and probably extend her life a few weeks or a few months. My mother was terminally ill, and her death in the near future was inevitable. It was better to do everything possible rather than give up.

My mother wanted to have the second operation. She commented, "You don't know until you try." When she came out of surgery, she was doing better. Her condition surprised even the surgeon, although he believed this was a temporary and not a long-term improvement. I was sleeping at my mother's house and driving back and forth to the hospital to be with her. One morning before I went to the hospital, I received a call from a retired Admiral friend. He said he was sorry to tell me I was passed over for promotion to captain. I appreciated the courtesy call from the Admiral rather than finding out in some other possibly embarrassing situation, but I was really angry. I thought I was not being promoted because of the wreck, because of the presumed effect of my tragic personal losses. I did not want to tell my mother, but when I went to the hospital that was the first thing she asked me. She knew the Selection Board was meeting the previous two weeks.

When I told her what happened, she was angrier than me. She told me I should try again, that I should not give up. I told her it would be more difficult to be considered a second time because I was passed over now. I would need a much stronger record than the first time. There was only twelve months before the next Selection Board. I told my mother not to expect too much. This could be the end of my promotions. She adamantly disagreed, and said, "Find out more about what really happened and what can be done about it. Do not give up." I quickly agreed with my mother, mostly because I thought she was too sick to be bothered with my situation. I wanted to change the subject to topics to help her rest better and use her energy to work toward improving her health.

As I was driving back to her house for another night's sleep, I started thinking she might be right. She was usually very perceptive about politically packed matters. She was soon strong enough I could return to Miami and leave my mother with professional caregivers. She wanted to go home, not to a nursing home. My sister Alice, whose husband Bill was a medical doctor in my hometown, made arrangements so my mother could be at home and get the help she needed. My mother was doing better as soon as she got home, and I made plans to come back to see her again as soon as possible.

Meanwhile, I found out who was on the Selection Board. It was really a discovery about who was not on the Board. There was no one I knew and no one I had worked for. No one on the Board was looking at a fitness report they wrote about me. The luck of the draw was really terrible. I thought it could not be that bad twice. Mom might be right. Keep trying. I also realized my first fitness report as Commanding Officer of the reserve unit would not be due until October, 1985, so I had not received any benefit for promotion purposes because there was nothing in my record yet. I started thinking about what else I could do to improve my chances. The first thing was to keep working on the exercise involving the Straits of Florida, so I continued that work at my own expense. I attended the project staff meetings in Norfolk in June and July, becoming more familiar with Norfolk each time, but I was excused from the August meeting because my work was completed in July to await the actual exercise in September.

At the same time, my retired Admiral friend told me to become more active in the Naval Reserve Association by running for National Vice-President for Legal Affairs at the national meeting scheduled in Norfolk in early October. I began working on this. I made reservations and bought an airline ticket. I started lining up support within my district that included a major portion of the southeastern United States so I could be the district's candidate for this national office. During this time I continued to visit my mother on a regular basis. Although she was doing relatively well, she was now convinced she would die sometime soon. She wanted to repair everything around the house and gave me a list of things to do while I was there. She asked me to put fresh gravel in the driveway so it would not be muddy for visitors who would come for her funeral, and I did. She wanted the house to be clean, and it was, but she still seemed a long way from dying in August, 1985, even completing a new roof on part of the house that was damaged by a tropical storm the previous November.

As I was not going to Norfolk in August, I met with the other Navy Reserve Legal Unit in Miami and thoroughly briefed them on the upcoming Straits of Florida Exercise in September. This unit was composed of mostly senior officers (Captains and Commanders), and several of them volunteered to go to Key West in September for the Exercise. Everything about the Exercise was going extremely well, and I was encouraged by developments, remembering what my mother said earlier in May when I was disappointed. The Annual Conference of Navy Lawyers was being held in Washington in September during the week before the weekend Exercise in Key West that involved many reserves. At the end of the conference in Washington on

Friday, I made plans to fly back to Miami Friday afternoon so I could be in Key West Saturday morning.

I was attending the Annual Conference of Navy Lawyers because I was Commanding Officer of the reserve unit in Miami that supported the Military Justice Division of the Navy Legal Headquarters in Washington. The conference was very worthwhile with updates on numerous topics and explanations of recent changes and important court decisions. I participated in some workshop sessions on terrorism issues as I had done the reviews of the April, 1983 Lebanon Embassy suicide truck bombing while I was working at the Navy Headquarters in London during May, 1983. When the conference concluded, I was preparing to travel on a Friday when a tropical storm passed through the area and closed the Washington National Airport, stopping all flights in and out of Washington. I was stuck in Washington as the Exercise began in Key West Saturday morning. I telephoned the Commodore and was excused from attendance, but I did not have a good feeling about the situation. Once again, circumstances beyond my control were an insurmountable obstacle.

However, I continued preparing for the annual meeting of the Navy Reserve Association in Norfolk in early October. My local and regional support was beginning to solidify. I also learned that all was not lost in the Exercise at Key West as the Navy Lawyers from the other Miami legal reserve unit went to Key West and did the job as planned when I was unable to be there. I went to see my mother one more time at the end of September just before going to Norfolk. She was not doing as well that time but still insisted that I go to Norfolk. We talked, and she said, "I have been praying all of my life, and my prayers have always been answered." Two friends of the family that she named in my hometown also had cancer, and she said, "I prayed for both of them, and now their cancers have gone into remission. Why won't God answer my prayers and heal my cancer?" I said, "God will answer your prayers to heal you now, or He will heal you with a resurrected body, but he will answer your prayers and heal you one way or the other." She said, "I think that He will heal me this time by giving me a resurrected body because he is not answering my prayers for healing now."

I wanted to spend more time with my mother, but she insisted that I go to Norfolk to take care of business. She said, "Let me know what happens, and I will see you when you return."

I was not familiar with the Omni Hotel and the Waterside area where the national meeting of the Navy Reserve Association was held. I had never attended a national meeting of our professional association of Navy officers. I quickly learned the procedures and began visiting the regional caucuses to campaign as a candidate. There were two likely opponents based upon the information circulating around the convention, and I was the newcomer with no record at that level. The elections occurred Saturday morning, and I received the nomination of the Nominating Committee. When the election for my office was called, there were no nominations from the floor. I was surprised and relieved. The two likely opponents both decided not to run after all. I was elected without opposition which was a very good start for me. As the elections of national officers were the last order of business, I headed to the airport for my return flight. I called and left a message for my mother and then called again to confirm that she had received the message as she did not feel like talking.

At the Norfolk Airport, I spoke to some of other officers who attended the national meeting. These airport conversations were the beginning of my friendship with Roger Trifthauser and his family from Batavia, New York near Buffalo. On the return flight to Miami, there was an indescribably beautiful red sunset lingering for a very long time. I had the feeling something significant was ending that was symbolized by this spectacular sunset. As soon as I reached my house in Miami, I called my mother's house in hopes she would feel like talking, but I was told she passed away while I was on the flight from Norfolk to Miami. I asked about the circumstances and was told when she received the message about my good news from Norfolk she smiled and appeared happy. Then she turned over and went to sleep as she was staying awake for the news from me in Norfolk, but she never woke up again.

I felt a searing pain and a sense of silent, suffering solitude. Everyone was gone now. I was truly all alone with father, wife, daughter, and mother gone during a period of less than three years. My mother always prayed for me, and I felt a sense of vulnerability now without her lifelong prayer support to help me. I would miss her in many other ways. She took care of me with love, encouragement, and good advice as well as all the things she did for me that are more apparent when they are missing. I was miserable, but I prepared to leave for Cairo, Georgia the next morning for her funeral. She was seventy-five years old and had a very good life with many friends and many accomplishments. I was relieved she would no longer suffer pain in her new resurrected body, but I was devastated by her loss.

CHAPTER 23
MORE PRAISE

Negative developments dominated my life after I returned from London in May. My mother's health declined. I failed to be promoted. I received a non-pay, non-reimbursement of expenses assignment at Navy Headquarters in Norfolk. I missed the Exercise in Key West, and my mother died on October 7, 1985 before I could reach her one last time. My life resumed a downward direction. However, as soon as I returned to work following my mother's funeral, I received good news.

I was excused for not being in Key West for the Exercise. I would receive a Letter of Commendation from the Commodore for my work in helping get the Exercise organized and integrating international maritime law into an operationally successful plan fully protecting convoys in the Straits of Florida from hostile forces. I also received a copy of a very good fitness report from the Reserve Center Commanding Officer covering my first year as Commanding Officer of the legal reserve unit. Now I could compete for promotion!

In November, 1985, the Reserve Admiral from Jacksonville visited our reserve center in Miami and approved the plan I had developed to stretch reserve resources and cut costs at the same time. By combining two months of reserve drills in a Friday through Monday format in Washington, our reserve unit eliminated the backlog of cases and required reviews in the Military Justice Division. This plan was accepted throughout the region and spread across the nation within the Navy Reserve. Others claimed credit for this innovation. These claims of origination by others confirmed the effectiveness of the plan to enhance the contribution of the reserves to active duty performance.

I decided to spend my first Christmas alone by returning to London. I accumulated enough frequent traveler miles with Pan Am to fly first class and enjoy the trip.

London at Christmas time is very special and unique. The Christmas shopping is spectacular, but it is difficult to get a taxi because so many people come into London from out of town to shop. The days are very short. By Christmas there is very little sunlight. I spent most of the time with my cousin Patrick and his family including some of his wife's relatives. Although my special holiday time in London was enjoyable and relaxing, I was ready to return to the land of my first love, the land I always loved and served for many years. I had a very strong bond with America and appreciation for our uniqueness and boundless blessings from age fifteen when I returned from my first trip outside the United States in the summer of 1958.

Longing for home, I took an earlier flight from London to be ready for the New Year. I hoped 1986 would be much better than 1984 or 1985, the two worst years of my life in human terms. The quiet time between Christmas and New Year's at home was just what I needed to get reorganized, reoriented, and prepared for what was coming. I knew the Selection Board was meeting again in May, and I was advised to do something significant for promotion purposes. I got orders to return to Norfolk as the legal officer for another operational exercise to be deployed from Puerto Rico in the Caribbean. This added to my previous work in the Key West/Straits of Florida Exercise last September My participation in this new Operation Ocean Venture 86 Exercise was in the planning phase in Norfolk in April.

Most of my time would be spent at Norfolk's Little Creek Amphibious Base with the Exercise staff, but I would coordinate with the Legal Office of the top Navy Admiral in Norfolk. The Admiral was four stars while the Air Force General in command of the Joint Forces Exercise was one star. For training purposes, the Admiral wanted certain issues from the Geneva Conventions included in the Exercise relating to the law of war and humanitarian requirements in armed conflicts. The Air

Force General, originally a fighter pilot, balked. He wanted no legal stuff interfering with his exercise. He wanted to win the war without having to fight the lawyers. He saw two enemies, the enemy he would face in combat, augmented by our military lawyers.

I walked right into the middle of this high level inter-service hornets' nest rivalry. I needed protection fast to keep from being stung. I talked to the Captain in charge of the Admiral's legal staff. He came to tears as he told me about the issues. He said we had to find a solution or it would be all over for us. He was reporting to a full bore four-star who could blow everyone away in their Navy futures. The Air Force General was in a different chain of command. If he persisted in his point, the trouble could be terrible. The Captain asked me to resolve the impasse quickly before the end of the day upon returning to Little Creek.

I don't know where the idea came from unless it was from my guardian angel, but I immediately put forward my solution that I had never even thought about or known about before. Without any hesitation, I answered the Captain. "Why don't we simply go through the General's proposed operational order and pick out the situations we can use for our law of war training purposes instead of insisting we inject certain situations into his order?" The Captain instantaneously starting going through the order and counting the imbedded issues in the order we could use for our training purposes, without changing anything about the General's operational plan. We counted approximately thirty-seven situations built into the General's order we could use compared to approximately nineteen the Navy brass had originally wanted to push into the order. I was deputized to return to Little Creek and propose this compromise. The higher ups would not meet face to face or directly by telephone to save face and embarrassment if the impasse continued. I was being thrown to the high ranking wolves unless I was successful in my unusual diplomatic mission.

When I got back to Little Creek from Navy Headquarters, I found a high ranking member of the General's staff who was a Colonel in the Puerto Rico Army National Guard. The Colonel was very nice and seemed to like me. I presented the basis for resolution of the impasse to him. He liked the idea and said he would take the proposal to the General with a favorable recommendation. That was close to the end of the day, and I did not hear anything else from anyone until our big staff meeting in the auditorium the next morning. We waited a long time, and then the General walked in and presented his views on the Exercise planning. He said there would be no changes in the operational order for the exercise, but the law of war training would be conducted within the context of situations already existing in the operational order. The General said we would do all of the situations within the order. These were much more numerous than those originally requested by the Navy.

I was the most relieved person in the room. As soon as the meeting was over, I went to Navy Headquarters to report the results. My success in bringing about agreement was very welcome. The training was also improved by working with the realistic situations that were part of the exercise rather than including issues just for training that were not integral to the operation of the exercise itself. I was apparently successfully completing my assignment in Norfolk as I prepared to return home, an assignment I was told involved risk as well as potential reward for promotion purposes. I spoke with key individuals on the General's staff about my fitness report and submitted my input for the report. The Selection Board would be meeting soon for me, so I reminded key members of the General's staff not to forget about me in the whirlwind of deploying to Puerto Rico and running the exercise from there. As I was leaving Little Creek, our area was quickly becoming a ghost town as everyone else was departing for Puerto Rico.

I returned home and waited for a copy of my fitness report, but it never came. In spite of advice from my mother and Winston Churchill to never give up, I gave up. It was really all over this time. My second chance was gone! My record would be incomplete as the Selection Board had already convened. There would be a copy of my orders to Norfolk but no fitness report to go with those orders. I would be automatically disqualified because of the gap in my record. No one could speculate about what I did in Norfolk without knowing from a written report. I became reconciled to the inevitable final failure to be promoted to captain, and I focused on other areas. I was still Commanding Officer of the Reserve Unit, and I needed to finish my two-year appointment in September.

When the Selection Board finished its work and reported its results, I received a call from the Navy Reserve Association in Washington telling me I was on the promotion list. I was astonished and replied there must be some mistake because I was missing a recent fitness report. I was told again there was no mistake! The caller repeated, "You are on the list. I am looking at the list, Captain, and let me be the first to congratulate you on your selection for promotion." I knew my friend was serious and truthful, but I was still baffled. I asked him to find out who was on the Selection Board, and he read the seven names of the officers who served on the Board. I knew all of them except one, and I had worked for most of them. Several of them were looking at reports they submitted about my work for them.

It still should have been impossible if I had a missing fitness report. No one could rescue me from that situation, so I asked my friend at the Navy Reserve Association to find out about my missing fitness report. He said he would, and the telephone call ended with me in stunned silence. I was afraid to say anything for fear there was some flaw in the procedure. I could be embarrassed when my name was taken off the promotion list by way of correction. Moreover, confirmation by the Senate was still needed and would probably be several months in the future. I was trapped in uncertainty, afraid to celebrate for fear of making a fool of myself when it was realized part of my record was missing.

I waited impatiently and irritably for more bad news. Then an amazing thing happened. My friend from the Navy Reserve Association in Washington called again and told me, "The

Selection Board had your fitness report from Norfolk. There were no gaps in your record. It was noted by the Selection Board that your record was very complete and very impressive." I asked, "But how could that be possible? The General left for Puerto Rico without submitting a fitness report for me, and I never received a copy." Then my friend dropped his bombshell, bluntly explaining, "The General wrote the fitness report while he was in Puerto Rico running the Exercise. He had a courier deliver the report in person to the Selection Board in Washington. This made quite an impression on the Board. It was very dramatic, and the report was very favorable. Any other questions, Captain?" I thanked my friend and hurried to get off the phone so I could pray. I thanked God and asked forgiveness for doubting. My encounter with the angel proved true again. I was still on an assignment to become more involved in national defense.

I had a really great civilian business trip coming up in early June to Vancouver, British Columbia. I would kill four birds with one stone. I would attend the annual meeting of the Canadian Maritime Law Association, the annual meeting of the Canadian Marine Average Adjusters Association, an international maritime law seminar for continuing legal education credit and Expo 86, the international exposition on transportation and communication. With my future Navy promotion assured, I could really enjoy this trip and learn much that would be useful in my work. After changing planes and clearing customs in Victoria, on the final flight to Vancouver I noticed a lot of passengers staring at me. Another passenger laughed and commented, "You don't have any idea why everyone is staring at you?"

"No," I said, "can you tell me?"

"You are the double for our Governor of British Columbia, and you may have some difficulty because of that." I thanked him for the tip. The last thing I needed was to be blamed for someone else's actions.

When we landed in Vancouver, we had to clear customs again because our paperwork was not completed in Victoria. Sure enough I was mistaken for their Governor. I was able to clear this up after some explaining, and I was allowed to leave the airport. I got into a taxi and asked to be taken to the Hyatt Hotel downtown on Georgia Street. The driver said, "Whatever, you say, Governor."

I said, "But I am not your Governor."

And the driver said again, "Whatever you say, Governor. If you don't want to be the Governor for now, that's OK with me." That ended the conversation, and I was taken to the hotel. I checked into the hotel and went to my room on the 8th Floor. As I was getting settled, the fire alarm sounded. This was not a drill, and I smelled smoke. I hurried down the fire escape stairs and out onto busy Georgia Street wearing blue jeans and a white T-shirt just as I was dressed inside my room when the alarm sounded. I had not shaven since I left Miami many hours earlier. I did not look like a very solid citizen.

After the fire was extinguished, I could not get back into the hotel because the fire escape stairway exit doors locked behind us. I had to walk back around to the front entrance of the hotel and walk past all the people who were checking into the hotel for the same seminar and meetings that I had scheduled. Several friends recognized me and wanted to talk to me just when I wanted to slip by unnoticed. Many people that I did not know recognized me. The Canadians in the group were too polite to tell me I was putting on a bad show as their Governor. I finally got back to my room although I had to walk up another stairway where debris from the fire on the higher floors was being swept and washed down the stairwell. I had acquired a heightened appreciation for my room, and I was in need of prayer for the rest of my stay in Vancouver as well as giving thanks for my safety so far.

I felt I was temporarily free in Vancouver. My life was moving in a positive direction again. The pressure was off with the Navy for now with my recent selection for promotion. The seminar and meetings in Vancouver were very worthwhile and interesting for me, and the sightseeing was enjoyable. When the seminar and meetings were concluded, it was time to see Expo 86, and I moved to another hotel in the Bay Shore area of Vancouver closer to Expo 86. I rented a car so I could really get around. I took the car ferry to Vancouver Island and saw Victoria as well as the southern end of the island. I drove up the Trans-Canada Highway toward snow-capped Mount Baker that could be seen in the distance even from Vancouver. After some sightseeing in the edge of the mountains, it was time to return to Vancouver and focus on seeing Expo 86.

As a transportation lawyer, the Expo was especially important as well as enjoyable. The Canadians I met at the seminar and at their professional meetings were really hospitable, and some of them invited me to visit with them and go to the Expo. One family was very memorable, spending time showing me around the Expo. The father was a senior consultant in the maritime industries, and the mother fled from Estonia behind the Iron Curtain. The couple met in Toronto and married before they moved to Vancouver. They had two adopted daughters. The older daughter was a nursing student in college. The family was friendly and fun, but I ruined it all by not riding on the roller coaster that was everyone else's favorite fun at the Expo. The mother stated she was subject to motion sickness and stayed off the roller coaster with me while the others had a blast turning upside down and hurtling around the track in a blur, yelling greetings to us below. They were moving so fast I could not see them, but I recognized the voices.

When I went to the Soviet and Cuban Exhibits, the military significance was apparent. I realized there was another reason for me to be at the Expo that I did not know about when I went to Vancouver. The Soviet exhibit boasted that several hundred thousand workers died building a railroad into the permafrost area of Siberia. Not much changed from the time when Peter The Great built St. Petersburg on forty-four islands in the Neva River with hundreds of thousands of workers dying while constructing

Peter's Window to the West. The quality of workmanship in the cigars sold at the Cuban Exhibit showed a society with little incentive to do good work. Cuban type cigars made elsewhere were much better. The Cuban cigar Winston Churchill smoked during World War II as photographed when he visited Cuba no longer existed.

My time in Vancouver was coming to a close, and I responded to the hospitality of my "adoptive" family there by taking their older daughter to dinner at a very nice restaurant in Stanley Park. We were friends and talked at length, but there was no romance. She wanted to know more about the United States and Florida, and I wanted to know more about Canada. We also talked about many of the exhibits we had seen at the Expo as well as the entertainment there. There were several bands including native Canadian. We said goodbye as I was returning home the next day, but I never forgot the extra efforts of this Canadian family to help me heal as they learned of my tragedies.

When I went to the airport the next day to return to Miami, I encountered a somewhat familiar obstacle. I was again mistaken for the Governor of British Columbia, and I was temporarily delayed. As time passed, I was concerned I would miss my flight while waiting for a resolution of the mistaken identity, but the customs officer telephoned the Governor's Office and spoke with his secretary. I overheard him saying, "You are sure he is there in his office? You are looking at him now behind his desk? Well, OK, thank you." Then the customs officer sent me on my way home with his good wishes.

In July, there was another trip to a law of war seminar in Virginia. One of the presentations included showing videos of the Soviet atrocities in Afghanistan. As I was intently watching these videos, I was suddenly shocked to see some of the identical scenes the angel showed me during the encounter. I was overwhelmed by this striking visual confrontation confirming the accuracy of the vision the angel showed me during the encounter. As soon as the presentation was finished, I rushed up to the speaker and asked, "When were these videos taken?" His quick answer was "fourteen months ago." I instantly realized this was ten months after the wreck. These events that were captured on video were ten months in the future at the time of the wreck. The angel showed me the future, and now he was making sure I knew he showed me the future and that he was right about future events that had not occurred yet. I wondered when the other future events he showed me would occur and under what circumstances. What would be the extent of my involvement in these future unfolding times as stated by the angel?

After returning home in July, I heard my promotion group was confirmed by the Senate that same month, and my last trip to Washington as Commanding Officer of the Reserve Unit occurred in early August. After October 1, I would be in the volunteer non-pay reserve unit with several other senior officers. Then I could perform more active duty in Norfolk. For the past two years my primary active duty was in Washington along with my reserve duty because my unit was assigned there.

On the last day of my August trip to Washington, I was preparing to leave and saying goodbye to my active duty counterparts. I was taken completely by surprise when suddenly I was promoted on the spot. One of the officers came in with the order from the Judge Advocate General of the Navy, and the silver oak leaves insignia on my uniform were removed. The eagles' insignia for captain were pinned on. I was saluted and congratulated. It was a great day that was a long time coming. On my final flight home, I travelled as a Captain for the first time. It was a great experience that took twenty years of military service to realize. I did not know I would serve twelve more years. I did learn my official date of rank would be 1 January 1987.

The year 1986 was a much better year for me, and it was not over yet. I was sent back to the Navy Headquarters in Norfolk in November to work on some critical international issues including the Soviet submarine threat.

Later in July, 1987, I went to a national meeting of the Naval Reserve Association in Phoenix, Arizona where temperatures were hitting 127, but the indoor sessions were very informative. The admiral who was Chief of Naval Reserve was making a dynamic presentation about being prepared to fight and win wars with vitally necessary help from our reserve components. We could fight wars without the reserves, but we could not be sure of winning wars without help from the reserves. As he continued to talk, he seemed to look more and more like the angel. As he spoke longer, the similarity with the angel's appearance became ever more evident. I finally looked away. I was overpowered by this supernatural occurrence. The angel was dramatically reminding me about the unfinished business from the encounter and the visions he showed me. The effects of the encounter were inescapable. My life would never be "normal" again as it was before the wreck. I was now a man marked by a divine encounter with "work to be done on earth." As the angel said, I would work to make sure that the United States was "prepared to fight and win World War III" although I did not know what war that would be or when it would occur. However, I believed what the angel said that I would "not be taken by surprise."

I returned to Norfolk again in October 1987 to continue my previous work, helping contribute to containing or neutralizing the Soviet submarine threat. In October, 1987, the Captain in charge of the Navy Headquarters Legal Office in Norfolk told me it was time to move up to the Pentagon for my next duty in the Navy's International Law Division. I was looking forward to this as 1987 came to a close.

In October, 1987, I completed two years as National Vice President for Legal Affairs of the Navy Reserve Association (now the Association of the United States Navy). I thought that would be the end of my time as a national officer of our professional association as I was a lawyer. I had done the legal job while being promoted to Captain. There was apparently nothing left for me except to work as an international expert on special Navy assignments.

There were two good years, 1986 and 1987, that partially offset the bad years of 1984 and 1985. I was still hurt, but I had more hope now. I was grateful to those who befriended me in my time of trouble. The kindness of others had a healing effect during those years although my losses were still very painful.

CHAPTER 24
LOOKING FOR THE GIRL

On the flights home from Vancouver in June 1986, I was thinking about the encounter again. When I was trying to win my argument with the angel, he predicted I could have another family. I did not want to hear that because I wanted the family I already had. As a further challenge to the angel, I questioned, "What type of person would my future wife be, and what would she look like? How would I know she is the one I am supposed to have another family with?" The angel calmly replied, "If you want to see her, look over there to your left." I turned and there at some distance, I saw in a vision the profile of a young blond woman, kneeling, looking up toward Heaven and praying fervently. In the vision, what appeared to be bright moonlight highlighted her profile. I saw her from a side view, but I did not communicate with her. In an instant, she vanished from view while I was still trying to argue with the angel.

I lost my argument with the angel, and I primarily focused on other aspects of the encounter for two years after the wreck, but now I realized everything about the encounter was coming true. If this was part of God's plan for me, possibly I should be looking for the girl. Besides being the one God has in mind for me to have a new life with, maybe she had some needs I was supposed to help her with. Maybe I was wasting time when I should've been moving forward with my life and helping her with her life. So I started being more conscious of this part of the encounter with the angel. I became more alert observing others, thinking I could sometime unexpectedly encounter the girl in the vision. I knew she was a real person, and she was out there in the world somewhere. When I became frustrated and impatient, I tried to find someone special on my own, but it did not work. I kept thinking about the girl in the vision.

I saw her praying. That was my only clue to her real identity. I began to focus on church groups and church activities, thinking this was more likely to bring me to her. Without realizing it, I was making a mistake similar to father Abraham. I knew God's plan, but I was trying to get control of it myself. Toward the end of 1987, I recognized the truth. This situation must be left in God's hands. I was driven by my encounter with the angel because he was correct about everything else, but I was apparently going nowhere in this area. As 1988 began, the girl in the vision was still nowhere to be seen.

CHAPTER 25
UNEXPECTED ENCOUNTER

In April 1988, I was surprised by an unexpected short-notice invitation. Muffin's mother asked me to attend a fundraising dinner that night attended by hundreds of people for a pro-life pregnancy center founded in affiliation with Rev. Billy Graham's National Christian Action Council. I was very interested but could not go. When I declined the invitation, Rosalie Elliott was very disappointed. Then she explained why she was inviting me.

"I want you to meet the young lady who is the Executive Director. She is truly outstanding and a strong leader. I was with my friend Sonja Ryskamp for lunch today. She knows this young lady Raymie Pardue very well and supports her ministry. She wants to introduce Raymie to someone really nice. I told Sonja I was thinking about someone to introduce to my son-in-law Bob Bell. I think you are ready to meet someone special after almost four years of being alone."

I was really interested, but I still could not go. This sounded like a God thing! Muffin's mother and her friend who was a Federal Judge's wife were acting as matchmakers for Raymie Pardue and me. I was certain this young lady would be a praying person as she was intensely involved in the spiritual warfare related to a ministry with very high-stakes life and death issues. I learned she was very attractive with light colored blond hair. She was sick recently for an extended period of time and recently resumed her responsibilities as Executive Director.

I suggested we could meet some other time. Rosalie promised she would see what could be arranged, but it would not be a date situation. It would be some group occasion where we could just be introduced to each other. Raymie was protecting herself from a dud introduction. Our first meeting would take some time before it occurred. It would require a suitable gathering to provide the desired setting. After several weeks the expected event emerged, the late afternoon singles' luau of Granada Presbyterian Church where Raymie was an active member.

The location was the lakeside Snapper Creek Estates home of Judge Kenneth Ryskamp and his wife, Sonja. Their backyard sloped from the house down to the water's edge. It was the perfect setting for a mostly outdoor gathering in South Florida. I did not see Raymie outside. She was in the kitchen talking to the hostess, but she came outside and sat down on the grass nearby. There was another girl talking to me. I was not trying to make Raymie jealous, and I did not know the other girl, but I did not want to be rude in front of Raymie. There was some limited conversation with Raymie. She said she had been sick and was leaving early to rest. When she left, I walked with her to her car in front of the house.

I tried to talk to her as she walked through the yard to her car. She responded she would be out of town visiting her parents in Baton Rouge and was not sure when she would return. I felt I would need some sort of breakthrough to successfully follow up with Raymie. I waited impatiently until I heard she was back in town. She was still recovering from an illness, and I recalled my own experience using large doses of time-release vitamin C to help me recover. I decided to take her some time-release vitamin C from the health food store. This would give me a reason to visit her office to bring it to her. It was after lunch when I arrived, and the receptionist was a volunteer lady, Ampara Ross. I asked if I could see Miss Raymie Pardue for a few minutes when she would not be too busy. I waited nervously while trying to look relaxed and friendly.

I was finally shown to her office. She was puzzled why I came to see her. I explained about the vitamin C and how much it helped me to recover. I wanted to bring her some of the same type of vitamin C as it could help her, too. It needed to be kept in a cool place, preferably refrigerated. I brought it to her personally so it could be kept at the correct temperature and would not be left out in the South Florida heat. Raymie's attitude toward me seemed to change although she was still somewhat reserved. After a short conversation, I said I realized how busy she was, and I did not want to take up too much of her time at work. As I left, she walked to the front door of the office and said goodbye. I felt I might have better luck after this meeting if I called her later.

I learned much later from Raymie what happened when I left her office. As soon as I was gone the lady at the reception desk asked Raymie, "Who is that young man?" Raymie told her I was not important. I was just someone she met at a church event. Ampara Ross replied confidently, "Well you will be married to that young man in six months." This led to vehement, angry denials by Raymie, and then the office returned to taking care of business. When I called Raymie later, she was agreeable to seeing me and was much friendlier.

I picked her up at her apartment. We were riding in my car as she explained her illness mostly affected younger people. I commented I was not young enough to worry about that illness. She looked really shocked. I realized she thought I was much younger, possibly around fifteen years younger, but we continued talking. She had a very strong moral character and was a committed Christian working to save lives and souls. We talked about the famous runner who would not run in track meets on Sundays and the biblical basis for pro-life beliefs.

She seemed very close to the girl in the vision I saw during the encounter with the angel, but something was different. She looked different. Her hair was different. I am not sure what else was different. Maybe she was older now. I learned she prayed earnestly, and we continued to be friends, getting better acquainted. One Saturday, I suggested we drive to Flamingo in Everglades National Park. This was a great outing. It was not too hot yet in May. During the late afternoon drive back to Homestead from Flamingo, the sun was setting to our left. Raymie fell asleep in the front passenger seat while I drove. The last rays of the late afternoon sun struck the left side of her face.

Her hair was pulled back. At that moment, she suddenly looked exactly like the girl in the vision. The last fading rays of sunlight had the same effect now as what appeared to be moonlight in the vision. It was completely uncanny. I was staring at the girl in the vision on the front seat of my car right beside me. The light shining on her face looked the same as the light in the vision for a few moments and then quickly faded away as it did in the vision.

My gaze was totally riveted on her. I froze at the steering wheel. I was startled to realize I ran off the road on the right side, but I managed to bring the car completely back onto the pavement. Raymie woke up because of the noise and the car shaking. I looked shaken. She knew something was wrong. I made some excuse about a wild animal in the road I dodged to keep from hitting it. She did not believe me and wanted the truth. I suggested we stop at a restaurant in Homestead as it was dinner time. I decided to simply tell her the truth over dinner. She would either believe me or never want to see me again. I felt she should know the truth whether she could accept it or not. How she responded would confirm if she was really the girl in the vision.

I was amazed when she believed my account of my encounter with the angel and the vision although she had questions about some of the details. Her grandfather and an uncle were pastors. She knew about spiritual matters and was involved in ministry herself. She did not think I was crazy because of my encounter with the angel and the vision.

Then it was time for me to go to the Naval War College in June. The long distance calls from Newport, Rhode Island set new records. I asked Raymie to come up to Maine and meet me after I finished my assignment. She invited her friend Daisy from New York to go with her. They stayed at a different place in Bar Harbor while I stayed at the Bar Harbor Motor Inn. We met for sightseeing, and I showed them around as I was there several times before.

We saw the towns of Mount Desert Island and Acadia National Park from Thunder Hole to Jordan Pond to the top of Cadillac Mountain with its spectacular views of Bar Harbor and Frenchman's Bay nestled far below. We took boat rides from Southwest Harbor and ate lobster, clams, and blueberry pancakes at the Mary Jane restaurant in Bar Harbor. The ice cream in Maine was the best with maple, fresh blueberry, strawberry, and other genuine flavors. The Fourth of July Parade was just getting started as we left Bar Harbor to drive to Boston's Logan Airport, but we had work schedules to resume after the holiday. So we boarded our flights at Logan, Daisy to New York and Raymie and I to Miami.

At last we were alone and could seriously discuss the subject of marriage. Raymie said yes, and I was on "Cloud Nine" at 31,000 feet as we cruised to Florida. Raymie wanted the wedding at Granada Presbyterian Church, and she agreed to wear my mother's diamond platinum ring. That was my mother's wish when she was dying. My mother wanted me to marry and have another family, and she wanted to have a part in the wedding even though she would not live to see it. She said that would give her peace that her family would continue. (I was an only child of my father's second marriage as his first wife Ruth died when he was the same age as me when Muffin died.)

Later in July, we visited Raymie's parents in Baton Rouge and met their huge extended families at an old fashioned southern home reception for us hosted by their family. Raymie's mother was one of eight children, and her father was one of five. There were many more new names than I could absorb so quickly. We returned to Miami and continued to make arrangements for our planned October wedding. Raymie was in charge of almost all of the planning details except for one major matter.

CHAPTER 26
A MILITARY WEDDING

I wanted a military wedding, and Raymie liked the idea. I contacted my retired Admiral friend in Miami. He said he would get permission. I was within the scope of the regulations. I was a senior reserve officer. I was promoted to Captain over two years earlier. I finished two years as National Vice President for Legal Affairs of the Naval Reserve Association and was currently serving as National Parliamentarian. My Navy career might be coming to a close. Our military wedding could be the grand finale that we could enjoy immensely, setting our wedding apart and making it especially memorable.

The officers of the South Florida legal reserve units agreed to participate in the wedding and form the customary arch of swords for us at the conclusion of the ceremony. One of the officers who was a lawyer could not participate because he was in a different type of unit, but he let us use his membership at the Coral Reef Yacht Club on Biscayne Bay for our rehearsal dinner. My Navy family was closing ranks all around us as I was embarking on a new life with Raymie. As our wedding date of October 8, 1988 approached, we planned our honeymoon. Raymie did not want to travel far as we would be tired after the wedding, the reception in the church social hall, and all of the preparations and activities leading up to the wedding.

I suggested the Grove Isle Club Hotel. It was on a small island in Biscayne Bay. There was limited access across a small private bridge from the nearby shore in Coconut Grove. I purchased a temporary membership in the Club, allowing us to make reservations for the hotel and have access to the Club's restaurants. We could look across Biscayne Bay a short distance to the shore line of Coconut Grove, and there was a path along the water's edge so we could walk completely around the island. There was also a small store at the island's marina where we could buy supplies and souvenirs.

On the day of the wedding, I left my dress white Navy uniform in the choir's dressing room at the church. I drove my car to the Grove Isle Club and valet parked. I took a taxi the short distance back to the church and put on my dress white uniform for the wedding. All of this was completely secret. No one had any idea where to find us or my car. My new father-in-law Raymond drove my second car to the church as a decoy, but everyone was still looking for my other car that was hidden. My new mother-in-law Joyce told me Raymie was having a bad hair day. She stated, "I know you are not supposed to see the bride before the wedding on your wedding day, but if you want to get married, you need to go find Raymie and convince her she looks great."

I quickly complied. It was an easy request to fulfill. Raymie looked absolutely wonderful. Her hair was exquisite along with her dress and everything else about her appearance. We proceeded with the wedding as scheduled. It was a beautiful ceremony in a lovely setting with flowers and foliage everywhere. The church was very traditional in architecture and style. At the end of the wedding ceremony, we kissed and walked out together through the huge double doors at the front of the church. The Navy officers in their white uniforms were just outside the front doors of the church and formed an arch of swords for us to walk under as we left the church. Someone surprised, exclaimed audibly, "They have an Admiral in their arch of swords." I thought what is really important is Raymie is under the arch of swords with me, and we are married now.

The arch of swords and the gathering on the front lawn of the church to see it were assembled at a busy five-pointed intersection in Coral Gables where it was quite a spectacle. Amid the screech of brakes and skidding tires, several cars almost wrecked looking at us. The photo op was cut short as we were apparently a safety hazard to passing traffic. We walked around the outside of the church to the social hall for the reception while order was being restored on nearby roads. Several of the legal officers joked with me that they wanted to break ranks and rush over to the passing cars to offer their professional cards to potential accident victims amid the traffic melee.

The reception and the receiving line were terrific. Many friends and relatives expressed their congratulations and best wishes. The Ryskamps were unable to attend, but another Federal Judge was there. I worked for him as court-appointed counsel in a lengthy criminal case nine years earlier. It was impressive he remembered and came to our reception. The most memorable detail about the reception was when we were photographed cutting the big wedding cake with my Navy Sword. We also had Italian ice cream from a company owned by one of Raymie's church friends.

As the reception was finishing, it was time to change clothes and make our get-away. There was still an ongoing search for our get-away car. It was expected someone would drive our car to the door at any moment to pick us up. There was surprise and some disappointment when instead a limousine pulled up to take us away. As we quickly left, massive amounts of bird seed (instead of rice) were thrown at us and dumped on us. The church specified bird seed as it was more ecological. The birds would eat it, also easing the clean-up burden on the church. The limousine took us to The Grand Bay Hotel restaurant for our first dinner as a married couple. After dinner we went to check in at The Grove Isle Club Hotel, still shedding more birdseed with every step and movement for several days.

We were successful! Our destination was still a complete secret. No one was able to follow us. Raymie called her mother later with contact information so her mother and family would not worry. We stayed at the Grove Isle Club in seclusion for several days and had a wonderful time. We walked around the island and sat outside at the restaurant overlooking Biscayne Bay and its boats. Our new life together was off to a great start, and we would be travelling together in the near future. It was terrific being on our honeymoon so close to home and yet seemingly so far away and secluded.

Bob and Raymie immediately after walking under the arch of
swords shown above

Bob and Raymie cutting their wedding cake with Bob's Navy
sword, October 8, 1988

CHAPTER 27
WORKING AT THE PENTAGON

After our honeymoon, October at home was gone before we realized it. In early November, it was time for the meeting of the Maritime Law Association of the United States on Marco Island. The head claims manager from the Lloyd's claims office in London and his wife were flying to Miami and wanted to travel overland from Miami to Naples and Marco Island to sightsee. Ron and Maureen were delightful and charming. They arrived in Miami late afternoon from London and spent the night in a hotel to rest. The next morning Raymie and I picked them up for the drive to Marco Island.

We drove on old U.S. 41 across the Everglades. Ron and Maureen never saw this before and were fascinated with the endless expanses, airboats, and Native Americans. We stopped at the Miccosukee Indian Village to sightsee and so Ron and Maureen could buy gifts and souvenirs in the village store. A Miccosukee man wrestled a huge alligator, turned it over on its back and put it to sleep. Ron and Maureen were amazed. We saw it before, but we were still impressed by this fantastic feat of human courage and determination to overpower a much more powerful predator.

We stopped across the highway at the Miccosukee Indian restaurant to have a lunch of Native American food including "Indian Bread." Ron and Maureen were having a great time, and they often repeated "jolly good" and "lovely." We continued to Marco Island through the Big Cypress Swamp and arrived at our hotel to check in before dinner. Marco Island has a beautiful beach on the Gulf of Mexico. Although this was a working meeting for Ron and me, it was like a second honeymoon. Raymie and I could be together, and the business meetings were relatively low key. There were social activities including spouses and for spouses.

Time passed quickly. We were soon driving to Miami to get ready for our trip to Washington later in November for me to work at the Pentagon in the Navy's International Law Division. This was my first duty at the Pentagon after working in Norfolk for four previous assignments from 1985-1987. We planned to stay at the Army and Navy Club on Farragut Square just north of The White House. We wanted to drive to Washington because Raymie does not like to fly and so we could see Williamsburg.

As we drove to Washington, we turned off at Richmond to reach Williamsburg. The weather in Williamsburg the first night was unusually cold. We sat in the outside portion of a restaurant for dinner. We were almost frozen. The local people were not bothered by the cold weather. We warmed up as we left after having hot food and hot drinks. While leaving, we noticed several very athletic, very well dressed men packing very heavy semi-concealed heat. We thought they might be Secret Service agents because they were so heavily armed. We thought they might be clearing the way for the President or Vice President. State police cars also arrived, and we thought it might be the Governor of Virginia. We decided to sit in the cold on a bench in front of the restaurant to see the arrival of the very important person.

We waited a very long time. Nothing happened! We waited for what seemed like forever while we discussed our creeping frostbite. At last, a big charter bus pulled up, and a delegation of foreign businessmen got off with their cameras and binoculars. Now we saw our long-awaited celebrities. We laughed at ourselves as we rushed indoors to a warm place for the night. The President, Vice President, and Governor were never on the agenda. We jumped to an entirely mistaken conclusion, but the "grease guns," partially hidden under the overcoats of the security men, looked very convincing.

After the weekend in Williamsburg, we drove to Washington to check in at The Army and Navy Club so I could be ready to go to work early the next morning at The Pentagon. We looked forward to enjoying Washington from our location just north of The White House. We would celebrate our first Thanksgiving together. We were thankful for our new God-bestowed life together. We were thankful for our nation and for those who had gone before us in its service. We also saw the Club's exhibits commemorating our history and those who served. It was a third honeymoon in less than two months except I had to be at work at 7:30 every morning in the Navy's International Law Division at the Pentagon.

It was relatively quiet in Washington. The weather moderated so we could get around town and see The Capitol, The White House, and many other famous historic landmarks including a tour of The Pentagon. Ronald Reagan was finishing his second term as President, and George Bush was elected earlier in the month, awaiting his inauguration in January, 1989. The Administration would basically continue but with a new President as George Bush was Vice-President for eight years under Ronald Reagan. At The Pentagon no major changes were expected. It was mostly a situation of getting the work done that was already on the agenda and continuing to make progress in many areas.

For me, working in the International Law Division was the result of twenty years of working toward that goal after receiving my Commission as a Lieutenant Junior Grade in early June, 1968. It was exciting to be working in an area where I had real world experience outside the Navy as well as many related assignments in The Navy before finally moving up to The Pentagon. I did all those things a newcomer does. I researched issues and wrote memos about treaties and international agreements involving current issues. I researched the laws, cultures, politics, and economies of other nations where we had plans to negotiate agreements or plans to update existing agreements. I worked on immigration issues where we had citizens of other nations who volunteered to serve in our armed forces. This was especially inspiring where individuals came to our defense even before becoming citizens.

My previous experience working on international issues at the Navy Headquarters in London was especially helpful now. Some of the same issues were being worked on higher up at The Pentagon. My initial work at The Pentagon prepared me for future work there. I could return later and immediately be immersed in current projects and issues.

Our November "third honeymoon" trip to Williamsburg and Washington was coming to an end all too soon. Before we left Washington, we had tickets for a tour of The White House while Ronald Reagan was still President. Raymie and the President earlier corresponded because they had the same February 6 birthday. Raymie wrote the President who supported pro-life issues to wish him a happy birthday and to say she would be praying for him. The President replied saying he noticed they have the same birthday and to thank her for her letter and her prayers. We did not get to see the President. He was out of town, but it was thrilling to end our time in Washington with a tour of The White House and to see how it looked as arranged and decorated by him and Mrs. Reagan, including their china dinner set.

Leaving Washington, we drove down the Appalachian Parkway to see mountain scenery. We gave up on this venture as all the restrooms along the Appalachian Parkway in Virginia were closed for the winter. Pioneer practices were hilarious, but indoor plumbing was preferred. We returned to Florida to prepare for our holiday trip to Baton Rouge where I would be the newest member of the family. Time passed quickly as we finished packing for the trip.

We attempted to drive to Baton Rouge in one day, but after we passed Mobile, we encountered very heavy fog and had to stop in Pascagoula, Mississippi for the night. The next morning we turned on the television news to help us get going. We heard the terrible news that the Pan Am flight from London to New York was bombed over Lockerbie, Scotland with all aboard dead. I was very upset. In the past, I travelled on that same flight. I was also very angry that nothing effective was done to stop terrorism. I was having a flashback to the Embassy bombing and the Marine Barracks bombing in Lebanon in 1983, and now it was happening again.

We composed ourselves and continued to Baton Rouge. There was nothing we could do now except be thankful we would be safe for the holidays at home with family and friends. This was our first Christmas together, and we were going to enjoy it.

CHAPTER 28
SUDDEN STORMS

In 1988, I was appointed National Parliamentarian of the Naval Reserve Association. I was also elected to serve the following two years as National Vice-President for Legislation and began several years of working on issues involving Congress. The angel was continuing to be correct with his comments about my future. In August 1989, our first child Emily was born, continuing to fulfill the angel's promise that I could have another family. Six weeks later Raymie had emergency surgery because of a condition related to her pregnancy with Emily, but God protected Raymie and restored her health consistent with the angel's promises.

In July 1990, I stopped over in London for business on the way home with my family after an international conference in Paris in June. Emily was ten months old. Emily's cousin Ashley and her Aunt Shari went with us. Following the international conference in Paris, peace seemed secure. Germany was reunited politically on July 1 with economic union to follow on October 1. The sinister shadows of World War II in Europe were receding when Kuwait was invaded by Iraq in August 1990, followed by Desert Shield and Desert Storm.

After desert victory earlier in 1991, the Naval Reserve Association elected me in September 1991 as National Executive Vice President (in line to be President). Our second child Jeremy was born in November 1991. Events were moving along on the path promised by the angel. In the national defense arena, I worked against cuts in the Navy Reserve with help from Senator John McCain and other "navy" senators. After success in fighting the cuts during the summer of 1992, I returned with my family from vacation in Branson, Missouri. On August 24, 1992

Hurricane Andrew struck with full fury and almost no warning. The storm quickly intensified to a super record breaker crossing the warm waters of the Gulf Stream to hit us. Jeremy was almost nine months old as our family, Cousin Ashley and Aunt Shari sheltered in our home seeking safety from the savage storm outside that killed at least thirty-seven people in our county.

Conditions were deplorable in the aftermath of the storm with extensive damage and debris and no electricity. We worked for one week to minimize our losses until nothing more could be done. Raymie and her sister and the children evacuated to a hotel in Central Florida. While my family was safely evacuated, I travelled separately to attend the national meeting of the Naval Reserve Association in Chandler, Arizona. I talked to Senator John McCain at the head table about our national defense issues and family news. He was there to speak to our group.

This national meeting was different. It was smaller, and some areas of our nation were not well represented. Because of the ferocious hurricane and its impact, I was almost the only delegate from Florida. On Saturday morning I saw there was trouble, but it was too late to get enough of my supporters to the meeting. On a quick motion from the floor, I was dumped as a national officer, apparently ending my rising role in national defense. When I arrived at the Phoenix airport, I was met by a car and driver, but now it was difficult for me to get any ride at all back to the airport. Finally, someone felt sorry for me and squeezed me into an already packed car. I wanted to ask the angel what happened. This was not part of the plan as stated by the angel in the encounter.

I would have to re-assess everything. I was very discouraged, but I did not have time to mope. I returned home to continue picking up the pieces from Hurricane Andrew. I had to restore my business and repair our house. Other matters would have to be put aside. It was three weeks before electricity was restored and many months before business could recover. At least my memory of my encounter with the angel still encouraged me in this situation. God was helping us get through something terrible at home even though His national defense role for me was recently thrashed in Arizona.

CHAPTER 29
POLITICAL PARADOX

Thinking my national defense service was ending, I looked for other ways to serve. The governmental response to Hurricane Andrew was overwhelmed by the magnitude of the mess. There was federal help, but the state itself could have been much better prepared and also better equipped to coordinate the response and recovery. Florida is a very high risk state for hurricanes, so we should not have been surprised. I saw the need for a central "war room" at the state level to coordinate efforts to always be prepared and ready to respond. The state could also divert some of its already budgeted expenditures into disaster areas to boost business recovery there at no additional cost to the state. Limits could be placed on the growth and size of upper level bureaucracies to place more resources in the field to help people following natural disasters. This concept could also be applied to regular state programs such as education, emphasizing classroom teachers rather than a burgeoning bevy of bosses ensconced in palatial buildings.

Remembering what the angel said about helping others, I became a candidate for governor in January 1993. I campaigned all over the state discussing the issues raised by the recent hurricane and the overall effectiveness and efficiency of state government. If I was not elected, I could still call attention to these issues and help push for improvements. Other candidates might absorb some of these ideas to increase their appeal. I recall speaking at an event in Pensacola. A man spoke to me after the program was over. He said, "Hurricanes are a South Florida problem. We do not care about that in Pensacola." Of course it is very much a statewide problem, and I was saddened years later when a major hurricane struck Pensacola, a city I loved where I worked years earlier as a civilian employee of the federal government.

After Hurricane Andrew, there was an upsurge in respiratory illnesses. This situation persisted for many months after the storm because of the atmospheric pollution and debris stirred up by the storm. In February 1993, Raymie developed life-threatening pneumonia and was rushed to the emergency room with a dangerously high fever. The emergency prayer chain at our church was activated in the middle of the night, and Raymie's fever broke when the prayer warriors went into action. Her condition was still critical, but God protected her and restored her health over time, blessing her with follow up treatments from a pulmonary specialist who was really good.

As I continued to campaign around Florida for most of 1993, I noticed I met people who were interested in national defense issues and who encouraged me to be involved in that area. I also heard there was discontent with the officer who replaced me in Arizona. I was encouraged to come to a national meeting in Seattle in the spring prior to the fall national meeting for elections in October. At the Seattle meeting, I saw more evidence of discontent with the officer who replaced me. I was encouraged to run again in October.

This was an uphill battle. The other officer was the incumbent now, and he would not be taken by surprise because this was the regular election cycle and not the "off year" meeting that occurred in Arizona. His group was also hosting the national meeting in October in their home city, and they were doing a very good job. There were four candidates for national president including me and the officer who replaced me. There was a runoff between me and the officer who replaced me. When the votes were counted, the other officer was announced as the winner, and his celebration began. I noticed his celebration was mostly a small group of his close friends at two tables together. I thought there were not enough happy people, and I was thinking of asking for a recount. At that moment, a lady from the credentials committee where the votes were counted rushed over to the podium and handed a note to the Parliamentarian. He gasped and exclaimed, "Oh, no, there has been a terrible mistake, Captain Bob Bell is your new National President." This time the celebration was more widespread. More people were happy, and I thought about how God overruled at the very last moment to place me back on track for a bigger role in the arena of national defense issues.

Now I was in the middle of a political paradox. I should not solicit support in the governor's race from military and veterans individuals because I was now representing them. It could be a conflict of interest, and my national defense role would come first. I was also an active reserve, and my state campaign diminished as I became more involved again in national defense issues. I was cut off from over two million veterans and military retirees in Florida because I was fighting for their interests at the national level. I could not effectively wear two hats. I would wear the hat the angel gave me for national defense.

Magazine front cover with Bob's photo as National President

CHAPTER 30
A NEW MISSION

Toward the end of 1993, something else happened that pushed me back into the international arena and into helping someone in a much more personal role. In a miraculous manner God called us to find and adopt our younger daughter in Ukraine. From September 1993 through most of 1994, we worked against obstacles to Caitlyn's adoption. I had a new mission now. Between the ongoing adoption process and my newly elected job as National President of the Naval Reserve Association, I was pulled away from the state campaign as if by a powerful angelic magnet. As we continued into 1994, it became more likely it would be the best two out of three for me, the adoption and national defense, and probably not the state campaign.

Things were heating up in the national defense arena with weapons systems and equipment issues. There was the big overriding human issue that the troops were not receiving pay increases and cost of living adjustments like the federal civilian employees. This was discrimination against our defenders of freedom, and our national defense could be seriously undermined by a flight of talent is this situation continued. Wars are won by dedicated and courageous individuals who should not be victimized by political irresponsibility. I worked throughout 1994 on these issues writing editorials, getting resolutions from the Naval Reserve Association, and networking with other military and veterans' organizations. I constantly reminded everyone that national defense is the main job of the federal government, "to provide for the common defense."

I advocated more effective defense strategies, avoiding wars of attrition and bringing conflicts to a conclusion quickly with overwhelming conventional forces and maneuver warfare against enemies to lower our casualties and costs. Where we could be drawn into longer, more major wars, I advocated not throwing away our hard-won victory by premature and complete withdrawals. World War II and Korea showed that without occupying other nations, we could keep some bases there on a cooperative basis to stabilize situations and avoid recurrences or re-matches of earlier conflicts.

At the same time, our adoption of Caitlyn was a major uphill battle. Ukraine was closed to international adoptions as confirmed by our State Department in Washington and the Ukraine Embassy where they laughed in our face for even asking about adoptions from Ukraine. God kept pushing us in the direction of the adoption. Our daughter was found and identified by a mission group from our church. They brought back photographic evidence that they found our "Bell-looking child" in an orphanage in Odessa. This was Raymie's test to find our child. It was amazing how much Caitlyn looked like the baby pictures of Emily and Jeremy, but our friends told us nothing could be done about adopting her.

I was adamant that all things are possible with God, but others felt it was hopeless. Caitlyn was a medically needy child with a heart condition. There was no time to waste. She needed major medical attention she could not get in Ukraine. Through a very unusual chain of events, God led us to an American lawyer in London who had an office in Kiev. He said he would help us. He had very high level contacts in Ukraine. He said he would have more credibility because he was not an adoption attorney. This would be a special case assisted by his high level contacts who were assured by him after checking us out that we were honest and sincere with no ulterior or improper motives.

The months dragged on with the immigration process, first U.S. approval and then Ukraine approval. In June, everything was on track to finish soon when there was a last minute snag. The adoption could be a political issue in Ukraine elections because of abuses that occurred with other international adoptions from Ukraine. Our case was very different, but we were feeling the heat from the prior misconduct of others. Our attorney called to say it would take a miracle to get our adoption back on track. When we went to the prayer meeting at our church that evening we asked our pastor and the elders if we could pray that the high-ranking official in Ukraine who had approval authority would not be able to sleep until he signed the decree approving our adoption. Our pastor said we would only be praying for the man to have a very active conscience. We would not be praying for anything bad to happen to him.

We organized in groups of four to pray four hours each during the usual sleeping hours in Ukraine that are the normal awake hours in Florida because of the major time zone difference. Two days later, our attorney called again saying the decree was signed approving our adoption. He reported the high-ranking official called him to come to his home to sign the papers. When our attorney arrived at the government official's house, he found the man unshaven, pacing back and forth and complaining that he was unable to sleep for the past two nights. He said, "I want to sign this decree so I can get some sleep and be able to face the elections in two days."

Later in the summer, I was called to come get Caitlyn in Ukraine. I left with a friend, George Roller, in early September, two days after my participation in the Florida election was finished. There was still a considerable amount of unfinished business in Ukraine concerning the adoption. The administrative procedures and court appearances consumed two weeks in Odessa and Kiev accompanied by intensive prayer support from Florida. Whenever there was an obstacle, we telephoned home to ask for more prayer support. Caitlyn was now twenty-two months old. When we first found her, she was eleven months old. Her adoption process was non-stop for eleven months.

With permission to leave Ukraine obtained, more miracles escorted us home and smoothed our path back to America through Warsaw and its U.S. Embassy where Caitlyn was processed. Upon arriving with Caitlyn at Miami International Airport in September, there was a joyous reunion with family and friends.

We received VIP treatment coming through Customs, but I was tired after almost three weeks of non-stop effort away from home.

Raymie took over, and Caitlyn's first open-heart surgery was scheduled as soon as possible in December 1994. The operation was state of the art at that time. We have the same blood type, and so I gave blood to contribute to Caitlyn's transfusions. Our pastor and others from the church came to the hospital and prayed with us during the surgery. The operation was successful, and the long process of recovery began.

CHAPTER 31
PREPARING FOR WAR

The Republicans took control of Congress in the November 1994 elections. The new Congress convened in January, 1995. I was working on the long-awaited pay raise issue for military personnel and other defense issues. With the Clinton White House and the Republican Congress, national defense was a bi-partisan issue where both parties wanted to claim success. My work from the previous year suddenly gained momentum in the new "it takes two to tango" Washington political scene. My home front was stabilizing with Caitlyn improving gradually and getting additional medical help that she needed.

This was my last year as National President. I would soon meet my goals or face failure and pass the torch to someone else. The Naval Reserve Association networked with other military organizations. I wrote editorials for our magazine and worked behind the scenes. If our ideas were accepted, a huge base of support would be mobilized.

The planned USS George Washington was not funded. The Administration and Congress did not want the construction and constant operational costs of a huge 10th nuclear-powered aircraft carrier cruising the world's oceans with a full crew complement. Nine was the absolute limit. When this issue was discussed, there was consternation. The need for the 10th carrier was clearly shown, but congressional cost containment was king. It was the end of the George Washington before its beginning.

I remembered what the angel said, and I felt it was not over. I remembered what my mother said about not giving up. I applied my reserve rationale to the issue. I decided to agree with the limit of nine active duty nuclear-powered aircraft carriers but asked that the George Washington be built as a reserve carrier.

This would avoid a very expensive continuing active duty crew and operational costs. The George Washington would be in port as a training facility for reserve personnel and active duty crew members for the nine active carriers available for sea service. This would involve a small fraction of the personnel, fuel, repairs, and maintenance costs compared to full active-duty use. There would be the one-time construction cost, and the appropriations issue would recede to a reserve matter. There was doubt about this type of costs concession on the issue, but no one had any other possible approach to propose. This alternative was therefore advanced as a compromise.

There was not much hope for success as we waited for the congressional reaction. Approval came quickly to the surprise of everyone with their muted mutterings of amazement. This was unbelievable, but the angel was right. My national defense efforts suddenly gained momentum. The next barrier to be broken was the approval of the long-awaited pay raise for millions of active duty, reserve, and retired individuals. President Clinton sent me a letter as President of the Naval Reserve Association confirming the passage and implementation of the pay increase, and I sent him a letter thanking him for his support. Both letters were published at the same time in the national magazine of the Naval Reserve Association. This was cause for celebration. Over three years were consumed before the military pay was increased or adjusted for the cost of living. Civilian government employees received increases and COLA's during those years.

This was considered the ultimate achievement of my career. The conventional wisdom was that there was nothing left for me to accomplish. This was it. I introduced the Chief of Naval Operations to speak at the reception of the Reserve Flag Officers Conference in Washington in April. I introduced the CNO again in June at the Strategy Seminar at the Naval War College in Newport, Rhode Island. The CNO again acknowledged me several times, thanking me for my efforts. As a previous Chief of Naval Personnel, he understood the importance of retaining trained, experienced, and dedicated men and women. We were not merely "human resources" like trees in the forest to be cut down and not replaced. We were people who meant business in the defense of our nation. The President of the Naval War College invited me to breakfast at his house on base along with another admiral who was on track to be Chief of Naval Reserve. I realized that admirals personally appreciate pay increases like anyone else with the added multi-dimensional aspects of keeping their force structure of real people intact and always ready.

What appeared to be completion for me was actually the prelude to the grand finale that God was orchestrating. Congressional authorization for construction of the multi-billion dollar 3rd gigantic Sea Wolf hunter-killer submarine was going nowhere. In defense circles, this was viewed as the insurmountable issue. I wrote an article pushing for the submarine in March, but it was not published then. In August I was in Washington for active duty at The Pentagon, and my article finally appeared in our magazine. The authorization legislation passed the House of Representatives, but the votes were not there in the Senate. However, the situation suddenly changed, and the authorization narrowly passed in the Senate with several Senators who had opposed it all along now voting for it. This seemed to be an unexplainable fluke, a mistake. That evening over dinner at The Army and Navy Club with a relative, the question how it happened was a topic of conversation but remained unanswerable. As we were leaving, we stopped outside at the front entrance to talk for a few more minutes about family updates. Suddenly, a congressional staffer passing by addressed me as "Captain Bell." I was baffled. I did not know him at all. I replied, "Yes, but when did we meet?" He responded, "I recognized you from your photograph in the magazine. I read your article about the Sea Wolf submarine. I was researching the issue for Senator Dole. He asked if there was anything new before he voted against it. I showed him your article. After he read your article, he changed his vote to support the authorization. Another senator who usually votes with Senator Dole changed his vote.

This assured passage of the authorization that would certainly have failed without your article."

I was dumbstruck. I thanked him for his kind words. I realized only God could cause what happened. The 3rd Sea Wolf submarine tipped the balance of forces in our favor. No other nation could compete with us in a submarine arms race. We would rule the depths of the waters, the surface of the seas, and the airspace over the oceans. Our Navy would keep the peace with overwhelming superiority.

After years of efforts, I finally reached the national defense summit the angel foresaw in the encounter long ago. I was returning home from my final active duty at The Pentagon, and the next month in September at Providence, Rhode Island, I would be finishing my two years as National President. There was no time left for further developments in Washington involving me. It was almost over now.

CHAPTER 32
RETIRING FROM THE NAVY

The next several years were working mostly at the U.S. Southern Command in Miami in its legal office. I had to face the facts I would soon be retiring from the Navy with thirty years commissioned service and two years prior enlisted service in other branches of the military for a total of thirty-two years, but I was not ready to quit. I asked to stay longer. The Admiral who was the Deputy Commander of U.S. Southern Command wrote a letter asking that I be extended beyond my normal retirement time. The Navy could not grant his request. If any exceptions were made, it would open the floodgates for applicants asking to stay longer. The Navy had to stay within the force levels authorized by Congress and retire more senior officers to make room for others coming up through the ranks so younger officers could be promoted. New blood is the lifeblood of the Navy and the other branches of the military services.

I realized as the angel said in the encounter I would need to make the best use of my time. There was work to be done during my remaining time in the Navy, and I would need to take advantage of the available time and opportunities. It was rewarding for me to work at the U.S. Southern Command on matters close to my heart and always on my mind. From the Arctic to the tip of South America, the Western Hemisphere was home, and we needed to make it a higher priority. Our friends and neighbors should receive more attention, and arrangements for military cooperation would strengthen disaster relief and elected governments throughout the Western Hemisphere.

One of my assignments was to work on establishing military cooperation with Mexico, our closest Latin neighbor. This would involve some joint exercises with our forces and theirs and a wide range of military to military cooperation. Like the country studies I did at The Pentagon including several Latin nations, I studied the situation carefully and compiled information and recommendations to help in meeting and negotiating with our Mexican counterparts. I had done some civilian business in Mexico, primarily involving its Gulf ports and Mexico City. I had also visited Monterrey in northern Mexico and the Yucatan in the south with it historic Mayan ruins. I used my understanding of Mexico to outline an approach to maximize our prospects for success in establishing better relations and a new framework of mutual cooperation. I also found books providing more information so we were not just relying on our own experience and common sense. We utilized broader sources of insight and knowledge about our important neighbor with whom we share a long southern land and river border.

Our efforts were successful. We secured direct joint military cooperation with Mexico for the first time since the Mexican War. Everyone was very pleased, not only at the Federal level in Mexico but also within its twenty-eight states. We extended our cordial commitment to cooperate with them and work together on matters of mutual concern and humanitarian response to disasters. I thought my work was almost finished, but God had one more assignment for me. In April 1998, within three months of my scheduled retirement from the Navy on July 1, 1998, a hemispheric conference of high ranking military officers was held at the Southern Command in Miami. Most of the nations in the Western Hemisphere were well represented. This was the grand finale for me professionally in the Navy. God saved the best for last for me.

After the conference, I was busy finishing my work. In June, I went home for the last time from the U.S. Southern Command. However, it was not completely over just by departing for the final time. I received a letter of appreciation from President Clinton and some military certificates covering my service. A retirement party was planned in October 1998 during fleet week at Port Everglades, Florida. Captain David D. Welch was also retiring and planned this event aboard the USS Cole, a ship commissioned earlier at Port Everglades when Dave and I were there with others. There were three of us who were retiring including Robert L. Andrews who was a judge in Fort Lauderdale. The hospitality of such a large, modern ship with so much capability was amazing. When the ship was commissioned, there were so many people attending the ceremony that sightseeing aboard the ship was not practical, but now we were shown around inside the ship and invited into the Captain's wardroom to wait comfortably until it was time for the retirement ceremony and the festivities on the rear deck of the ship.

Raymie, Emily, Jeremy, and Caitlyn enjoyed looking around the ship before the retirement ceremony. One of the pastors from our church, Carlos Salabarria, came and said a prayer. It was a beautiful setting high up on the open rear deck of the ship overlooking the anchorage, the port, and the other ships. This was our final salute and farewell. We now realized in our hearts and minds what was already official. The ship's crew was extremely courteous and considerate of all of our needs. The entire occasion was memorable and provided a distinctive closing to the chapters of our lives in the Navy. As the American flag waved in the breeze and a band played, we looked back over our past service that was now concluded. When our final interlude of Navy time aboard the USS Cole was over, we went ashore to one of the port buildings where a first class reception was organized by our efficient friend and fellow retiree Captain Welch. As the sun was setting over the still waters of Port Everglades, we said our last goodbyes and headed for home to stay. My thirty years in the Navy Reserve was now fully behind me, twelve years after I originally planned to retire (before the wreck occurred in July, 1984). I was now actually retired after serving twelve more years than I planned because of the missions I was given in the encounter.

We did not realize that the USS Cole with all of its awesome firepower and advanced technology was vulnerable to a terrorist attack from a small boat packed with explosives that was brought alongside the ship by militants. The Cole was docked at Aden in Yemen on the Red Sea in the Middle East on a peaceful, friendly, goodwill port visit, "showing our flag" when the terrorist attack occurred. The explosives blew a hole in the side of the Cole where the enlisted dining room was located when many sailors were there. We were especially saddened to learn that many of the thirty-seven sailors who died in this treacherous attack were the same ones who had hosted our retirement ceremony aboard their ship in Florida.

These young sailors showed so much kindness and consideration to us. They showed their skills and prowess as well-trained sailors with bright futures in the Navy and beyond. Their loss was heartbreaking and underscored the continuing terrorist threats that affect all of us. We settled back into our civilian lives while our thoughts and prayers continued to be with those who were still serving and with those and their families who sacrificed so much. I watch closely from the sidelines now and keep a personal vigil for those who still serve and protect us while we live safely and comfortably at home.

Bob receiving the folded flag flown over the U.S. Capitol at the retirement ceremony

Raymie receiving spouse recognition at the retirement ceremony

From left to right, Bob and Raymie with their children Caitlyn, Jeremy and Emily at the stadium for Game Six of the World Series in 1997 (Florida vs. Cleveland)

CHAPTER 33

MOVING ON

December 1998 and January 1999 were the first Christmas and New Year's holiday season in thirty-two years when I did not have any military obligations or duties pending. The children were old enough to enjoy the holidays with relatives in Baton Rouge. We were happy. We counted our many blessings, giving thanks to God.

After the holidays, I realized God was re-shaping my life. My volunteer work at Granada Presbyterian Church was taking more time and becoming more urgent. I served as an Elder for four years, and I was close to completing a second four years. During this second term, I was Clerk of Session. I presided over meetings of the Elders and the Congregation. I kept a record of actions by the Elders in our regular, periodic, or called Session Meetings.

When the Senior Pastor was leaving to become pastor of another church, my job suddenly intensified. I was elected to the Pastor Search Committee and was asked to be Chairman while continuing as Clerk of Session. This was more than the time demands of my military involvement. The Pastor Search Committee met frequently. We prayed. We wrote letters. We contacted prospective pastors. We visited their churches to meet them and hear them preach. This involved significant travel. The greatest distance was going to visit a pastor near West Point, New York. The Military Academy was beautiful, overlooking the Hudson River from a high bluff, just as my father, a former Cadet, described it.

It was a very long process lasting almost two years. Our interim pastor continued the work of the church while we searched. We prayed as a group with everyone joining in individually. It was a very powerful experience repeated many times. We prayed, and we waited. God was forcing us to take our time and not rush our mission.

After I retired from the Navy in 1998, the decline in my civilian business accelerated. There were a few large cases that were costly to handle and dragged on for a long time, but the volume of small and medium-sized claims continued to drop. Without a larger volume of conventional claims, a high level of quality service could not be maintained long-term. The downward trends were apparently irreversible because of permanent changes. Ports elsewhere in Florida and along the Gulf and lower Atlantic coasts developed extensively with improved facilities. South Florida no longer had such a large share of the cargo business.

There were also fewer claims because overall port security and the security of sealed cargo containers improved. Computers mapped out new, more direct, and more economical shipping routes. Shipments no longer automatically left from or went to high profile ports of entry. The so-called "out ports" located along the coast between Miami and New Orleans and Miami and Norfolk were major factors combined with inland waterways. The clock could not be turned back to a type of business that was passing into history.

I was thinking about moving on and about where to relocate. I wanted to complete as many cases as possible before shutting down, and I wanted to finish the pastor search for the church. It would be amazing if everything finished at the same time. I believed God would allow the lengthy pastor search to conclude before moving me elsewhere. The new pastor would have a free hand with his "sponsor" gone.

Baton Rouge won because of the importance of family. Our children would know their grandparents and many other relatives in Baton Rouge. We would be part of a large extended family. My parents died before I met Raymie, so our children could not know them.

Toward the end the pastor search began to focus on Worth Carson. He felt called to our church, and he made a decision to accept our call. After much prayer we felt he was the one God had in mind for our church, and a congregational meeting was called to vote upon the unanimous recommendation of the Pastor Search Committee. This meeting was very well attended, and there was also some other business for the Congregational Meeting.

I was at the Congregational Meeting as Clerk of Session and as Chairman of the Pastor Search Committee. There was a moderator pastor from another church in our denomination. When it was my turn to pray with the congregation, Raymie stepped out of the meeting momentarily. I was praying during a pause in the meeting's agenda and asking the Holy Spirit to come and guide our meeting so our decisions would be pleasing to God. As I was praying for the Holy Spirit to come and enter our meeting, the huge, tall, heavy, very thick wooden doors at the rear of the sanctuary that were securely closed suddenly blew completely open.

It was a very clear, calm day in South Florida. There was no rain or wind. One of the deacons tried to push the doors closed again, but he could not! Raymie came over to help him, but they still could not close the doors. When I stopped praying, they were finally able to close the doors. The deacon wiped his brow and commented, "Whew, that was the Holy Spirit either coming or going."

When the votes were counted, the new pastor received 93 percent of the votes to concur in his calling as the new Senior Pastor. There was a special sense of peace now surrounding his selection. There was assurance he was the pastor God was calling, not just us as a congregation concurring in the pastor's own sense of calling to our church. The church was fortunately functioning as part of God's governance and not just under us exerting human decisions.

When we went to Baton Rouge for Christmas in 1999; we were looking for a house, We needed a house for a family of five and some pets with a home office area where I could work. From the time of the wreck in 1984, I continued to have a separate office area with a separate entrance in both houses where we lived. It was a fully equipped office, not just an alternative work area or a part-time facility. This kept me close to home and it was successful for seventeen years after leaving my 15th floor downtown office with its view of Biscayne Bay.

We found a house under construction to meet our needs. The house was scheduled for completion in May. We could plan to move in June when the children completed the school year. We returned to Miami and put our house on the market.

The pace of my remaining cases quickened. It seemed almost everything would be finished by June. The marketing of our existing home was apparently going well. In May, a "cash" buyer from Brazil with a family living in Miami came forward and signed a contract to buy the house. A closing was scheduled later in June to give us time to pack up and move, and the closing on the new house in Baton Rouge was scheduled a few days later.

We would be disconnected from Florida and reconnected in Baton Rouge very quickly. Almost all of my case work was rushing toward conclusion, and I made plans to close my law office at the end of June. I worked until the last moment to finish as much work as possible. We packed and left for Baton Rouge, but as we were driving just north of Orlando on the Florida Turnpike, the cell phone rang. It was very bad news. The realtor was calling to say the "cash" buyer's check bounced. The sale of our house in Florida was off.

We had already passed the point of no return. The fully loaded moving truck had gone ahead of us, and the builder of the house in Baton Rouge had our money. Our car slowed somewhat as we discussed our situation but then resumed a normal speed. There was really no choice. We still had to go ahead. We had to accept the new house in Baton Rouge and put our house in Florida back on the market. Perhaps our Florida house would sell quickly. There was another buyer we rejected because we already had a contract with our "cash" buyer from Brazil. When we reached Baton Rouge, the builder had trouble completing our house.

After several weeks, a closing was scheduled so we could finally move in as almost all of our belongings were on the moving trucks waiting to be unloaded. Our new dream house was turning into a nightmare. My upstairs office over the garage was not finished, so I could not work. I lost most of my remaining business in Florida because I appeared to be out of business rather than moving to a new location. When my office was completed after lengthy delays, the builder remembered to varnish the steps on the stairway leading up to my office area. I could not get back to work for another two days while waiting for the paint on the steps to dry. I remembered the old joke about watching paint dry, but it was not funny.

On the positive side, we got our children enrolled in Christian Schools. Emily and Jeremy were at one school, and Caitlyn was at another. I was busy driving the children to different schools in the mornings and picking them up from different schools in the afternoons. Caitlyn was on the waiting list at the other school, so eventually our children would be together.

Soon after the children started school, Emily was not feeling well. During the Labor Day weekend, Emily's condition worsened. By Tuesday morning she was very sick. We took Emily to the doctor, and as he was examining Emily and talking to us, he was telephoning the hospital for Emily's immediate admission for emergency surgery. Emily had appendicitis that developed to a very dangerous point. She was rushed to the hospital.

The operation was successful, but Emily was out of school for three weeks recovering. When she returned to her 6th grade class, the girls in the class nominated her for student council.

They made posters and campaigned for her for three weeks while she was out of school. The voting was scheduled that same day when Emily returned. When the votes were counted, it was a tie. All the girls voted for Emily, and all the boys voted for one of the boys. It was necessary to have a second vote, and one of the boys changed his vote to support Emily. This was the beginning of Emily's participation in student government. It was a positive development punctuating the excellent progress in Emily's recovery process. It was good news as we dealt with issues involving our new house and our house on the market in Florida.

I had one remaining case in Federal Court in Key West, Florida. I travelled there in October 2000 for a hearing. I saw Key West again where I had been many times including for Navy duty. I stayed in a quiet bed and breakfast inn one block from the Federal Courthouse. I walked to the Courthouse the next morning without worry about a car or parking. There was very little parking along the streets in the older, historic sections of Key West, so I took a taxi to and from the Key West Airport. Being in Key West again was a positive experience for me. One of my first successful civilian cases in 1970 was in state court in Key West representing the local newspaper, *The Key West Citizen*. I had friends and relatives in Key West through the years. Now I was back thirty years later for a final appearance.

The Judge was very cordial and considerate, taking extra time to consider all of the issues. At the airport leaving Key West, I visited with opposing counsel. We were opposed to each other so many times we were friendly. He was always courteous and reasonable in representing his clients. I pursued a similar pattern of professional conduct with him. It was good to have a long talk as our flights leaving Key West were delayed. I told him this was my final appearance. This was a good way to bring closure to my work in Florida. I departed from Key West and withdrew from my last case at the same time.

Our house in Florida was on the market for another year. Paying for two houses was dragging us down. The builder of the house in Baton Rouge was not responding, but there is a one-year new home warranty in Louisiana that applies to contractors and subcontractors. I spent most of the year working directly with the subcontractors on specific issues that applied to each one. There was one parts supplier who kept our money and applied it to the builder's account rather than delivering our parts to us. We refused to pay twice and used parts from another source.

On June 1, 2001, sixteen months after our house in Florida was first placed on the market, there was a closing. The sale of our home in Florida lifted a tremendous burden. With progress in resolving deficiencies in our new home, it seemed that our challenging transition was almost finished. There was more good news; our children would be in the same Christian school for the 2001-2002 academic year. There would be no more rushing back and forth across town to two different schools every morning and afternoon. Our personal lives were settling down into a more normal, stable existence again. I was working for the Lloyd's of London claims office, and I was also working on some local claims with Louisiana lawyers.

Even the weather seemed more favorable toward us. It was not the scorching, record setting prolonged heat wave we experienced the previous summer moving to Baton Rouge. There was local flooding in June from a tropical storm, but the water soon receded. There was not much damage, and we were not harmed. For us it was watching an unusual, record setting weather event. In mid-July I developed what I thought was a summer cold, but it did not improve. When I coughed, it was a dry, barking cough, but I could feel there was deep congestion. I started running a fever that did not respond to medications.

I was referred to a doctor who immediately diagnosed my pneumonia. He reassured me with his relaxed, joking manner talking about my "big old pneumonia." He quickly prescribed the medication and treatments I needed and sent me home for a lengthy recovery lasting six weeks. God placed me in the right doctor's hands, and my health was restored. I hoped this was the last obstacle to our resettlement that consumed over one year.

As I was recovering from pneumonia, I wondered if the encounter was finished. Our future in Baton Rouge was ahead of us. Would our lives resume without any further intervention from God related to the encounter? Our roller coaster relocation was leveling off as we counted our many blessings, including especially good health.

CHAPTER 34
AMERICA UNDER ATTACK

In September 2001, the weather was nice in Baton Rouge. Following a relatively mild summer, an early autumn seemed near. We were enjoying the serenity and stability of our new home. We were counting our blessings after a period of testing. Everyone was in good health again. I was enjoying taking the children in the mornings to The Dunham School nearby. On September 11, 2001, I was returning home after taking the children to school. It was after 8 a.m. Central Daylight Time when I walked into the house. Raymie was watching television and said: "There has been a terrible accident. A plane has just crashed into one of The World Trade Center Twin Towers."

I instinctively said, "It was not an accident," recalling some earlier work I was involved in with the terrorism issue. Raymie said, "Oh, you are always thinking like that. It was an accident. No one would deliberately fly a plane into The World Trade Center. Something must have been wrong with the plane." We continued to discuss our different opinions while watching television. Then in the middle of a sentence, another plane flew into the other tower. Raymie quickly said, "This is not an accident. This would not happen twice at the same place so close together." I said, "I know, America is under attack, and this may be just the beginning."

We talked about bringing the children home from school but decided to monitor the situation closely before bringing them home. Possibly they would be better off at school for a few hours where they would be shielded from the horrors that were unfolding as we watched people jumping to their deaths from the World Trade Center Twin Towers to avoid being burned to death. I remembered walking past the World Trade Center when it was under construction and asking how firefighting could occur in the upper floors of such tall buildings. I was told that a fire in the upper floors of one tower would be fought from the other tower using the other tower as a firefighters' platform to deploy water hoses and other equipment.

However, both towers were now ablaze at the same time, and the fires were out of control. Short of a miracle there was very little hope for anyone in those buildings unless they could somehow escape from the buildings. Those on the higher floors above the explosions and fires were certainly doomed. My anger level was steadily increasing as well as my compassion for the victims. This was the same terrorist threat I worked on in 1983, and nothing was done to effectively contain it or counteract it. The political will was apparently lacking to effectively defend America. The encounter was still relevant. We needed to be better prepared.

As the television coverage continued, we were informed that The Pentagon was hit by another plane. America was not only under attack, America was at war. This was far worse than Pearl Harbor. Both military personnel and civilians were being indiscriminately attacked, and the total loss of life would be worse than Pearl Harbor. I later learned that an Admiral and his wife who belonged to our Navy Reserve Association died in the plane that hit The Pentagon, a place where he worked. Another one of our members was piloting the plane that hit The Pentagon before the hijackers killed him and took over the plane. The Admiral who was Chief of Naval Reserve in his office in The Pentagon that day was the same Admiral who had breakfast with me and the President of the Naval War College at Newport in June, 1995.

When the Chief of Naval Reserve heard the explosion of the plane hitting The Pentagon, he rushed out of his office and headed toward the area of impact to render assistance. He was met by a fireball coming toward him from the secondary explosion of the jet fuel. He ran away from the fireball, but he could not run fast enough. He managed to duck into a side corridor as the fireball passed by him. One of my friends at The Pentagon had been spared, although I did not know it at the time.

Then, two things happened the terrorists did not anticipate. All flights in the United States were grounded, and all flights bound for the United States from abroad were turned back. Any airplane not responding to the no-fly order could be shot down and possibly prevented from hitting other targets that were on the terrorists' agenda. The other development the terrorists did not expect was when the passengers on a fourth flight over Pennsylvania learned about the attacks on the Twin Towers and The Pentagon. They realized the hijackers who took over their plane had similar plans although they did not know the intended target. It was apparently the United States Capitol Building that had not been evacuated. Congress was in session. The Vice-President was there, and First Lady Laura Bush, a former teacher herself, was there to speak on the educational issue of no child left behind.

The passengers organized. When Scott Beamer said, "Let's roll," they rushed the cockpit to retake control of the plane. When the hijackers realized the passengers were going to be successful, they crashed the plane into the Pennsylvania countryside. The passengers died, but their heroism and courageous actions saved our government from a possibly fatal blow. The terrorists did not anticipate that unarmed passengers would fight them to the death to keep other innocent people from being wantonly killed. The hijackers underestimated Americans. President Bush was in Bradenton, Florida in a school classroom speaking on no child left behind. He quickly realized America was under attack and at war. The no-fly order was issued. Evacuations were ordered for The Capitol, The White House, and The Pentagon in case there was a second wave of attacks. President Bush himself was secured in order to preserve the national command authority.

He boarded Air Force One and was flown to various locations until it was safe to return to Washington. More details about the attack on The Pentagon surfaced. The hijackers planned to hit the other side of the building but could not get the plane down low enough. They were taught to fly the airplane but not how to land it so they could not change their minds. They would die hitting their target or trying. They could not back out by landing the plane. They overflew The Pentagon because of their lack of training in altitude adjustment. The United States Capitol was directly in front of them, sitting on a hill, and it had not been evacuated as the attacks were just beginning. The Capitol was not their target, it was assigned to another plane. They were determined to follow orders. They were determined to get to The Pentagon and knock out America's military organization.

At the very last moment, they turned and banked the plane to the left right in front of the Capitol, heading back toward The Pentagon. The White House was right there in their path. They did not know President Bush and Laura Bush were not there, but everyone else was there because The White House was not evacuated yet. The White House was not their assigned target, so they flew past it on their way back to The Pentagon. When they hit the opposite side of The Pentagon instead of where they planned to attack, they impacted the one area of the building that was being reinforced and compartmentalized to be more bombproof. As a result, the explosions and fires, while devastating and deadly, were contained there and did not spread throughout The Pentagon to destroy it and cause even greater casualties.

Most of the people moved out of that area while the contactor was working. Some were already moved back in when the attack occurred. There was terrible loss of lives and friends in The Pentagon that day, but it could have been much, much worse. We still had the ability to fight back. Our military organization was not destroyed in a single strike as planned by the terrorists. The hard working people in The Pentagon immediately started working on plans for response options for President Bush. Then something happened that related specifically to my national defense role as commanded by the angel in my encounter over seventeen years earlier.

The 10th nuclear powered "new" aircraft carrier we were not allowed to count because it was used for training and for reserve programs was mobilized. Active duty crews were put aboard along with active duty carrier air groups (CAG's) and sent to the Indian Ocean on station close to Afghanistan. When the governing Taliban refused to turn over the terrorists they were harboring who had planned, manned, and directed the September 11 attacks, President Bush ordered air strikes by naval aviators and their planes from our 10th carrier. It was argued as not needed when I supported its construction in 1994, but the encounter was right on target. Although things were quiet for many years of human time, the national defense plan stated in the encounter had already been in place. Preparations were completed for a future time God could foresee. The naval aviators from the carrier conducted the first air strikes inside Afghanistan contributing to the fall of The Taliban within a relatively short period of human time. God's plan was in readiness all along outside of human time but always prepared to respond quickly to evil developments within our dimension of time and space.

I was called to come to one of the local television stations in Baton Rouge (WBRZ Channel 2, ABC Affiliate) to comment on the Navy's role in the war and on the international law issues that were involved. Col. Joey Strickland who was Director of Veterans Affairs for the State of Louisiana recommended me because he knew about my background. After the war shifted to operations from land bases in Afghanistan, it was more of an Army and Air Force endeavor. The Navy role and the international law issues receded from the forefront. I became a spectator again, watching developments on television like everyone else. My past personal involvement in national defense as directed by the angel in the encounter was confirmed again by current events, but my role now appeared to be over. Perhaps this was a sign that the encounter as it related to me was finally winding up seventeen years later.

There were still other terrorism issues in the Middle East. Iraq was harboring terrorists including the notorious Abu Nidal.

A book was written about him with the title, *The Master Terrorist*. Iraq was paying the families of suicide bombers who attacked Israelis. Iran was continuing to sponsor terrorism, but the focus was on Afghanistan. It was used as a base by the terrorists perpetrating the September 11 attacks. I followed developments closely, recalling our terrible tragedies in Lebanon in 1983. There was only a small group in a very small village on a mountainside east of Beirut, and the battleship New Jersey was in the harbor below poised for action. We could not get authorization to strike back then, and now a small group of terrorists in a tiny village in Lebanon had turned into thousands of terrorists with global reach, not limited to attacking us overseas, which was bad enough. They repeatedly attacked our homeland bent on more brutal, indiscriminate attacks without relenting or repenting, pursuing a diabolical policy of slaughter of the innocents to win by evil intimidation.

CHAPTER 35
HELPING OTHERS

All areas of the encounter relating to me personally seemed to be completed except the area of helping others. I could apparently take the initiative while waiting for God to lead me into more specific areas of helping other people. I was thinking of teaching and writing because I could reach more people to share my experiences. I enjoyed working on claims, but the number of people I could reach was limited to the number of claims I was handling. The people with claims wanted help with their claims. They were usually not interested in other topics, and my claims clients were a very small number of people or companies because some of them had more than one claim with me. I witnessed to others when my story could help someone. I shared one-on-one and in small groups, but my outreach was limited.

Raymie decided to return to teaching high school English in the summer of 2003 and was quickly hired by another local Christian school where our three children were enrolled. Raymie is an outstanding English teacher, and God suddenly improved our situation. Emily entered the 9th grade and was soon elected to student council. Jeremy was in the 6th grade, and Caitlyn was in the 5th grade. I was invited to come and talk to the 9th grade civics classes about terrorism. I had a PowerPoint presentation with photographs explaining how the terrorists attacked, showing their preferred tactics and their mindset. I focused on Lebanon in 1983 and Oklahoma City in 1995 to show similarities in the types of buildings that were attacked to achieve maximum destruction. I was much more familiar with the Lebanon situation but noted some similarities with Oklahoma City although it was domestic terrorism. While I was at the school talking to one civics class after another about terrorism, the teachers were talking about difficulties getting substitute teachers. I decided to help and volunteered as a substitute teacher.

Raymie was not sure I would be a real teacher. I did education and training in the Navy, but it was at the graduate and professional level for legal personnel. I never taught at the secondary school level, and I never taught full-time or part-time. However, I helped as a substitute teacher for a total of sixty-five days in a variety of high school and middle school classes including physical education. I remembered much that I learned in school. I did what the teachers asked me to do when I substituted as I did in the Navy. In May 2004 just before the end of the school year, one of the social studies teachers left with little or no notice. He was a football coach and was asked to be head coach at another school.

I was asked to take his place in the classroom for the coming school year. I could help with the classes because social studies was my strongest area. I was assigned to teach four classes of Western Civilization in the 10th grade and was asked to establish two World History Honors classes for the 10th grade. I would have 138 students in 6 classes, virtually every sophomore and a few from other grades. I wanted to raise the level of instruction in these history classes and include some of my real world experience in dealing with other nations and international matters. I had too many classes and too many students, but there was a high level of requests to be in my classes because of my experience.

I learned much more about history by teaching these courses. The early Greek historians Herodotus and Thucydides had different opinions. Herodotus believed God intervened in history while Thucydides believed man was alone, marching through manmade history. I agreed with Herodotus, not only because of my own encounter with the angel, but because the evidence from ancient times was so persuasive that God was interacting in history at key junctures. I thought the Hundred Years War between medieval England and France was the longest war in recorded history, but I learned there were several longer wars. The record holder was the war that lasted over 735 years between the Spanish and the Moors in Spain. Some would say this was a series of wars, but Spain was never completely conquered. The conflict persisted until the Moors were pushed completely out of Spain in 1492.

It was a privilege teaching my daughter Emily and her classmates. I finished my special year in May 2005. Another coach was coming in for these classes next year, and we were preoccupied with helping Caitlyn. Her earlier open-heart surgery repair was state of the art in December 1994, but eleven years later it was failing. It was projected to last five to ten years, so Caitlyn was beyond the outer predicted limit of her earlier surgery. Caitlyn had two eye operations in 1995 to correct lack of coordination between her eyes, three types of occupational therapy and counseling with good results over eleven years. Her eyes were working together, but she needed a second open-heart surgery for a pulmonary valve replacement.

Her pediatric cardiologist in Baton Rouge recommended the Children's Hospital in Boston. The Children's Hospital performed approximately two-thirds of all second open-heart surgeries where major issues developed after the first operation. The Children's Hospital is the pediatric teaching hospital of Harvard Medical School. It was on the cutting edge of advancements in the field of pediatric cardiology and open-heart surgeries. We had no hesitation in following the advice to go there. Caitlyn's cardiologist studied there and knew the doctor who would handle Caitlyn's case. We prepared for the trip, and we left with Caitlyn in July for our fateful journey to Boston.

On the verge of surgery, Caitlyn became very upset. She learned the therapy dog would not be available for her after surgery. This kept Caitlyn calm, looking forward to petting the dog as she had her own dog at home. Caitlyn became hysterical and wanted her brother and sister to be with her. I was told to go sit with her in the Hospital's beautiful courtyard/garden. She gradually began to calm down, and a clown came to entertain her from the hospital staff. After that the Hospital's child counselor came to see Caitlyn. She took Caitlyn into her office and helped Caitlyn tremendously with play therapy, toys, and stuffed animals. While entertaining Caitlyn, the counselor was communicating important information. Caitlyn calmed down and was ready for surgery.

However, the surgery was suddenly postponed until the following summer. There was a committee of fourteen doctors who voted to approve each open-heart surgery. We were surprised this committee deadlocked in a tie vote with seven doctors approving and seven doctors wanting more time before the surgery. We were very disappointed. It would be another year before Caitlyn could get relief. She would have to live with her condition and restricted activities until the medical committee decided the time was right. Our faith told us it could be better in the future. Technology was advancing, and Caitlyn's scheduled surgeon was in the forefront of new developments, so another year of waiting could produce a much better result. We saw the hand of God in the tie vote. The operation was still needed and would probably be done the next year.

I was still propelled by my encounter twenty-one years earlier. How could I help more people in my remaining years? I started working in August to help raise money for a new medical school to address the shortage of family medicine doctors in Louisiana. We were close to the bottom in that need category. I could be helping many people because of those who would be cared for by the new, additional doctors. I also volunteered in August to help develop an evacuation plan for New Orleans in the event of a major terrorist threat or attack, or a major hurricane. Although Federal grant money had been sent to New Orleans to develop an evacuation plan, nothing in detail was complete. The existing plan was to point everyone toward the roads going out of the city with no designated destinations or out of town facilities in readiness. Just go, every man, woman, and child on your own! New Orleans was like an "Old World city" with streetcars and other public transportation. Many people in New Orleans did not have one car per family.

My plan was to use the school buses. The children would be taken home from school, and then the school buses would pick up the people who needed transportation and take them to designated out of town destinations. If a hurricane was approaching during a weekend, the people could be picked up somewhat sooner because the children would already be at home. The school bus drivers would be paid for their help, and they would also be safely out of the city. This plan would be tied in with placing doctors in small towns. These doctors would meet the needs of the small towns and be available to help those who were evacuated or temporarily assist in New Orleans.

The height of the hurricane season was upon us, but it was difficult to create a sense of urgency in others when we requested support for this project. The Gulf hurricanes were quiet for many years. The last major lethal storm to lash the Gulf coast was Hurricane Camille in July, 1969. That storm hit the Mississippi coast instead of Louisiana. We met later in August with Congressman Richard Baker in Baton Rouge. He said he would help with establishing an evacuation plan, but it was too late for the current storm season. We needed to work on the evacuation plan over a longer time to get the Orleans' Parish school buses and drivers allocated along with some other buses. The medical care component of our evacuation plan would be more long range, dependent on educating more family medicine doctors who would agree to locate in smaller towns, rural areas, and in underserved urban areas.

CHAPTER 36
SUPER STORMS

Very soon after the meeting with Congressman Baker and very close to the end of August, a very large, powerful hurricane named Katrina appeared in the Gulf of Mexico and headed toward New Orleans. Most people were not old enough to remember anything except relative calm during hurricane seasons. Everyone was watching the picture of the storm on television. The weather commentators called it a perfect storm because the eye was so well defined and so tightly wound with a very low barometric pressure inside the eye. The storm continued its path toward New Orleans.

Emergency orders were issued, and evacuations began, but many people were unable to evacuate. They did not have transportation or money to be away from home. The poor and immobile citizens were left to their fate. Others who could leave stayed behind and trusted their levees to protect them. Surely this storm would be no worse than others that turned out to be false alarms. Many more affluent people left in their cars, treating it as an impromptu vacation. The storm was a real monster with extremely high winds and a huge storm surge. I recalled Hurricane Andrew and how quickly it strengthened to record levels. I was angry that the people were not better protected.

The storm passed just to the east of New Orleans on its way to destroy the Mississippi Gulf Coast with a direct hit. New Orleans was again spared a direct hit, and the next morning the television anchors were saying New Orleans dodged the bullet. Although it was early in the morning, there were already some celebrating their good fortune. Then the reports suddenly changed. Some of the levees were being overtopped, and water was coming into the city in some places. Doubt was expressed about the accuracy of these reports, but then the incoming information became even more ominous. Huge areas were being rapidly flooded. People were being trapped in their homes by the rushing waters. Many areas that were below sea level were now underwater.

How did this happen after the center of the storm with the highest winds and storm surge passed by to the East? The storm surge from the Gulf was flooding St. Bernard and Plaquemines Parishes south of the city along the Mississippi River, but where was the massive flooding in New Orleans coming from? The back side of the storm system was forcing water in from Lake Pontchartrain. The storm system was so large and powerful with its counterclockwise winds that the backwash from the departing hurricane now had much of New Orleans awash. This was a gigantic disaster with many lives lost and thousands of homes destroyed. The surviving people who had not evacuated were now being rescued from rooftops, but help did not come quickly. The magnitude of the catastrophe overwhelmed responsive resources.

In Baton Rouge we felt very fortunate. Other than loss of electricity, we had no damage. From Joyce and Raymond's house with electricity where we took temporary refuge, we watched in horror as survivors were scattered from the New Orleans area. Thousands of people were uprooted to go anywhere that was possible. We soon learned we were directly affected. We sold our house in May and moved into another house we were buying, but now the seller backed out. He said he needed the house for displaced relatives from New Orleans, but instead he sold the house for much more money in the inflated housing market following hurricanes Katrina and Rita. He kept our money and refused to extend the closing date as promised. In September 2005, there was so much chaos that business was disrupted. It was impossible to do anything until things settled down after the two monster hurricanes hit Louisiana so close together. We could not complete a closing in September. The seller was not cooperating. He lived in Lakeland, Florida. There was nothing we could do in the aftermath of the storms.

We would be homeless along with countless others unless we could somehow find a house in the superheated, oversold, inflated housing market after Hurricane Katrina. Houses were selling at the asking price before they were even listed, and many sellers were holding out for even higher prices. When we looked for housing, it was very discouraging, but Raymie somehow found a house we could lease. The owner was very nice and agreed to give us an option to buy along with a lease lasting over twenty-six months. This house was a real Godsend. It met our needs and was only two miles from the school. We moved in the day before Thanksgiving and finished moving just past midnight that Wednesday. We were there as Thanksgiving began, and Thanksgiving was very special. We gave intense thanks and counted our many blessings.

I thought this concluded our involvement in the detrimental aftermath of Hurricanes Katrina and Rita. The circumstances caused by the super storms halted the project to build a new medical school. We could not raise any significant amount of money. All available resources were going to hurricane relief. I was no longer active in this project by the middle of November. The time was not right following the colossal destruction caused by the super storms. Then something else happened on Thanksgiving Day.

Raymie's brother Jeff said I should apply for a job he knew about. I did not take his comment seriously at first. Jeff was working with a group of pastors, counselors, and funeral directors in the Joint Federal/State Task Force mobilized to look for over 13,000 people reported missing after the super storms, mostly from Hurricane Katrina in the New Orleans area, and to identify the mass casualties. I replied, "Jeff, I am not a pastor like you are, and I am too old. They are not going to hire a retired Navy Captain, and I am a lawyer. I am not a funeral director or a social worker." The Chaplains were very prominent in the task force organized by an Air Force Chaplain who retired and continued as the civilian director. There were medical personnel and DNA experts and technicians, but no lawyers. It was an emergency field operation.

Brother Jeff was persistent. He kept asking me if I submitted my resume, and I kept saying I was going to. One Monday morning in early December, Jeff called from work. "Bob, did you ever submit your resume?"

"No, Jeff, I did not think it would do any good." Then Jeff got on my case and said, "Bob, just e-mail your resume to this e-mail address I am giving you and call me to confirm when it's done. If I don't hear from you within an hour, I will call you again." I knew Jeff would not give up, and so I sent my resume, thinking that would be the end of it. The next day on Tuesday, I received a call to come in immediately for an interview, and I went because Jeff was on my case. By then I thought maybe I could help as I did some counseling in the Navy as a lawyer, but I was still very skeptical I would fit in with the organization and its missions.

After a brief interview at the Office of Volunteers of America on Government Street in Baton Rouge, I was hired on the spot to do telephone intake interviews and told to report for training the next evening on Wednesday at the Call Center operations building. When I got directions to the operations building, it was only two miles from the house we had just leased. The house was almost exactly half-way between our school and the operations center. I saw the hand of God in what was happening. I realized this was the encounter again. When the angel spoke about helping others, it was in the context of something of biblical proportions. God was going to use me to help thousands of tragic victims affected by the storms. God was in the process of clarifying the mission area in the encounter about helping others.

I went to training in the operations building and realized we were very close to the "war room" where the combined activity was located. As we were receiving instruction, we heard a bell occasionally ring in the war room followed by cheers from the workers. Someone asked our instructor, "What is that bell, and what is that cheering we hear?" The instructor explained, "That bell rings when another person is FOUND ALIVE. The workers cheer because someone else has been rescued from the hurricane and its aftermath." I was overwhelmed. This was another aspect of the encounter. God was saving people, and I would be used to help others in this time of terrible tragedies. Then the instructor showed us around the war room/operations center where hundreds of people were working long hours. We were told to report for work (twelve-hour shifts) the next day on Thursday.

The following morning I signed in early and headed for the telephone intake room where dozens of workers were busy at rows of telephones. This is where individuals were reported missing and where friends and relatives called in on a toll-free number with information about missing persons. As I was stepping across the threshold with one foot into the room, one of the supervisors tapped me on the shoulder and said, "Not so fast, didn't you do investigations in the Navy? Come with me." I was escorted to a large area nearby where dozens of telephone investigators were working at rows of telephones and computers and was told to be seated at one of the positions.

The supervisor said, "Help these workers. Most of them are from out of state, and start finding missing people now." God put me where he wanted me in a position to help many people. I did not know how many, but the projected numbers were staggering. I was re-connected with the encounter again even though I did not realize what was happening at first. It happened in spite of me and not because of me. I realized God put me in Baton Rouge ahead of time for this emergency situation just as He made it possible for the aircraft carrier to be built ahead of time so it would be ready when it was needed.

On Friday, I joined the opening prayer group that met every day at the beginning of the morning shift. Because the overall organization was under the Chaplains, there was no mention of separation of church and state, and there was never any suggestion that we should not be praying. These morning prayer times were very powerful and something I will never forget. As we moved through December 2005, there were still over 9,000 individuals who were missing as Christmas approached. I wished we could find all of them before the holidays. A truly daunting task remained because the people who were the easiest to find or identify were found or identified first. The difficulty of the mission increased as the number of missing and un-identified individuals decreased.

I was told I had a "sixth sense" in knowing how to locate missing persons, and I was frequently ringing the FOUND ALIVE bell and receiving cheers and applause. Soon it developed that every morning, I would be given a file on someone no one else could find and asked to locate the missing person before lunch. I became a trouble shooter on difficult investigations and had a perfect record solving the difficult case of the day every morning for more than a month. During this time I was thinking, "I can't win. Sooner or later there will be a case I cannot solve before lunch." I did not want to fail because my continuing success was encouraging others, and I was helping other telephone investigators with some of their cases. The dreaded day finally came later in January 2006. I was stumped. This one was impossible, at least in a limited amount of time, and it would require the combined efforts of several workers with varied areas of expertise.

This was a good time to take a short break and re-focus. My initial unbroken wave of success hit a barrier. I hoped this was not indicative of more tough cases ahead that could slow our overall progress that was spectacular so far. As I was walking toward the rest area, there was another tap on my shoulder. One of the big bosses stopped me and said, "You understand our process very well and know how to find missing persons. Come over here to the data processing area, and start reviewing these FOUND ALIVE files to make sure they were done correctly and correctly documented. Make sure they were really found and that we can show that." I was soon seated at a new computer in the data processing area. I was told if a file was not sufficiently documented to re-work it and re-investigate it so that we could show that the individual was really FOUND ALIVE. I received a "battlefield promotion." I was now in charge of internal review and corrective action for thousands of cases.

A major part of my method was to be a good listener. I realized that victims and those looking for victims needed someone to talk to so they could better cope with their losses and the convoluted circumstances. While helping them and taking their information, I was compassionate. I learned this after Hurricane Andrew. I let them talk it out, and more useful information resulted when they were able to talk without being rushed. I explained how the disaster occurred and how the response was organized. Many of them were confused or just lacked needed information. We eventually found missing persons in forty-four states and several foreign countries. The evacuations, rescues, and relocations caused by the super storms were the largest displacement of the largest number of people ever recorded from a single disaster. As I continued to work in the Joint Task Force (its name changed several times), I was proud to serve a state and nation where the missing and the dead were not forgotten and simply written off as a loss. Each one of the missing and the dead was given special individual attention and treated with dignity and respect.

As the months passed and the number of missing and un-identified dead continued to dwindle, in April we were again referred to Children's Hospital in Boston for Caitlyn's open-heart surgery. Her need for a pulmonary valve replacement was increasing, and this time the Hospital scheduled her in June, indicating her case had higher priority now. We began to make preparations throughout April, May, and early June. We would not make the same mistake this time. Caitlyn's brother and sister would be at her side. Her grandmother Joyce and her aunt Shari would also be there. Caitlyn would have full family support. Like the previous July there were many additional expenses, but the cost escalated now. Many people helped us raise money. Several groups at the school raised money. The workers in the Operations Center helped, and our church helped. I am not naming anyone for fear of leaving someone out because the support we received was very significant and broad-based including friends from out of state.

In preparing for our second effort at Children's Hospital Boston, we met with our pastor and requested prayer. He told us about the new technology being used to boost prayer participation and effectiveness. There was a website to provide us with a webpage for Caitlyn where we could post updates, and people could pray specifically throughout the operation as Caitlyn's situation was updated with interim reports from the doctors and nurses. This was a real breakthrough. When we contacted the Hospital to coordinate with them, we were informed the Hospital has the same service. We decided to use the Hospital's webpage because the Hospital had computers tied in with its system that we could use. Surgery updates would be in real time.

Many of my co-workers at the Operations Center watched Caitlyn's webpage during the surgery and prayed for her during each stage of the open-heart operation. One of the pastors at the Operations Center told me later he really got into praying for Caitlyn during her surgery, and he "felt her being healed." We knew the operation was very successful, using more advanced methods and technology than what was available a year earlier, and thousands of people from different churches and denominations were enlisted to pray for Caitlyn and her surgery. We felt that the massive prayer support was definitely a factor in Caitlyn's confidence entering surgery and in the excellent result achieved by the surgeon and his team. As Caitlyn and I had the same blood type, I again donated my blood for her transfusions.

When we returned to Baton Rouge, we learned something truly amazing that put the pastor's comment about supernatural healing in a new light. The cardiologist found that Caitlyn's heart showed additional spontaneous healing well beyond the excellent results of the operation. Caitlyn now had the heart of a healthy young athlete who was eating a good diet and exercising correctly with no indication of heart trouble.

This was a miracle that was not expected. We were praying for a successful operation, but some with greater faith were praying for miraculous healing. The cardiologist offered to make a CD of his scans showing before and after to prove it. The encounter showed itself again. The angel promised I could have another family, and no harm came to Caitlyn even though there was a twelve-year medical struggle leading up to the miracle. Caitlyn was in good health for the first time in her life with periodic checkups to confirm it. She was invited to Children's Hospital Boston in February 2007 to participate in a study. The doctors wanted to determine how such a good result was obtained in hopes of duplicating it with other patients.

At the operations center after returning from Boston, the number of missing and unidentified dead decreased to just over a thousand missing and about 300 un-identified dead. We were making our final push in July. When a missing person was FOUND ALIVE, this eliminated the need to obtain DNA samples from several close relatives to identify the dead. This disaster was different from others where DNA samples could be obtained by picking up the toothbrushes of those who were missing. The Katrina flood destroyed the evidence and the homes of the victims. Their close relatives and friends who could provide DNA samples and helpful information were scattered far and wide by the catastrophe.

Another factor emerged toward the end of the searches. There were apparently close to a thousand individuals who did not want to be found. They were taking the situation as an opportunity to make a fresh start in life, but we found them anyway and then left them alone, respecting their privacy and personal goals. The storm clouds had another "silver lining" that surfaced during our searches. Friends and relatives who lost contact were re-united after many years. Although they did not have the resources to re-connect with each other, we did through our joint task force. I personally held the record, re-uniting a mother and daughter in a tearful telephone reunion who had not been able to communicate with each other for twenty-two years. Others were similarly re-united after ten or fifteen years.

The joint task force was winding up and being de-mobilized in August, but I had reviewed the FOUND ALIVE files of over 8,500 individuals. I had completed, corrected, and updated over 3,200 individuals' files as part of the overall records of the joint task force. The Louisiana Family Assistance Center was shut down with close to 300 still missing and almost 100 un-identified casualties. These cases were returned to their local jurisdictions for further follow up. I was astonished at what God empowered us to accomplish in the year following the huge hurricanes. There are many untold individual stories of the workers and the victims. We "wrote the book" for this type of massive response. What we did and how we did it became the model for organizations in other states and cities to prepare for mass casualty and mass evacuation events.

I was ready for a rest, but I was also looking toward the future. After God's spectacular displays of His power and planning through many years, what was next? My curiosity about the future was heightened beyond previous levels. I would not make the mistake again of thinking that the effects of my encounter with the angel could be finished.

Family photograph, February 4, 2012. Bob and Raymie seated with their faithful dog Darla. Standing from left to right, their children Emily, Jeremy and Caitlyn.

CHAPTER 37
TAKING CARE OF BUSINESS

I was angered when I read in the local newspaper about a Fortune 500 company in Baton Rouge that really extended itself in responding to Hurricane Katrina and was now having difficulty getting paid for its work. During my work with the joint task force, I noticed many individuals and companies making money on our misfortune. They did not seem to have as much dedication to the tasks and as much heart for our unfortunate situation as individuals and businesses who were living through all the heartaches and hardships. I was incensed. A company that suffered its own losses and yet performed above and beyond the call of duty was being given the run around about getting paid by the Federal Government that was responsible for the failed levees and floodwalls.

I submitted my resume to see if I could help. I had forty years of experience in negotiations, settlements, and collections. I thought I could help the local company get its money. I had experience with Hurricane Andrew in 1992. What is needed most after such a disaster is business, customers, and cash flow. Insurance and FEMA pay to restore lost or damaged physical facilities over time but do not meet payrolls or pay ongoing expenses that can only be covered by jobs and a return to normal for businesses. Helping businesses recover is the great overlooked aspect of the aftermath of these storms. Raymie had doubts I would be hired. She thought the company I was looking at probably did not need any help. She thought they probably had everything under control, but I thought my righteous indignation on behalf of this company was related to my encounter-driven mission of helping others.

In the aftermath of Hurricanes Katrina and Rita, the company pumped the water out of New Orleans in the record time of slightly over one month compared to the minimum of ninety days projected by the U.S. Army Corps of Engineers. It was a visionary company with visionary leadership creating jobs for people in the aftermath of the storms. It was making worthwhile advancements for the public while making money to sustain itself. The company was a good corporate citizen, not just an opportunist raking in the money. I would be proud to help while it was benefitting so many.

I was called for a courtesy interview because of the references I listed. The interviewer later told me he planned to give me only three minutes as a courtesy to get rid of me to maintain harmony with my references. When we met, he suddenly seemed very interested and started asking me a lot of questions. He apparently did not want the interview to end, but he had only allowed three minutes on his schedule. As he escorted me back to the elevator, he was quickly talking to me and saying I should come back for further interviews with him and others in management in his division. As the elevator doors closed, he was still asking me questions, and I was still answering. He told me later that when we first met briefly he was startled when he suddenly realized the person he was looking for had come out of nowhere and was standing right in front of him.

I went back for four more interviews with the first interviewer, the legal counsel, the chief accountant, and the president of the division. I was hired and went to work in late October 2006. For over two years until February 2009, I led the charge to improve collections of accounts receivable, improve customer relations in the process of improving collections, improve cash flow, and improve cash on hand (money in the bank). My efforts took time but were increasingly more successful. While my work primarily benefitted my division, there were effects on other divisions of the company where they heard about what we were doing. I was willing to work with everyone. I did not turn anyone away because they were assigned to a different division. I was there to help others. I was still being driven by my encounter missions.

Without realizing it, I was helping prepare my division and the company for the impending recession. We were storing up money from the fat years to help the company survive the lean years that were ahead but that were not anticipated at that time. When the economic meltdown occurred in September 2008, at first we seemed unaffected. Business as usual continued into 2009 when the delayed effect of the downturn was felt. I was completing my assignment with the company. I projected three years with the company to complete my mission, but success came ahead of schedule. The individuals I trained would continue with better collections, improved customer relations, and sound business practices.

I thought about Joseph in the Bible storing up grain in the seven fat years for the seven lean years that followed in Egypt. I was certainly not in the same league with Joseph. I did not know what was coming, but I was glad I was able to help in a similar situation because my encounter assignments from the angel pushed me in the right direction. As I left the company, my life was close to taking another unexpected turn consistent with the encounter that was always with me.

PART III

UNENDING DIVINE
ENCOUNTER

I thought my encounter with the angel was a personal experience that would run its course when my assignments were completed, but I eventually realized the fallout from my encounter with the angel would never be over because my experience was part of eternity, meant for everyone, not just me.

CHAPTER 38
SHARING THE STORY

As time passed, my encounter with the angel was validated over and over again in so many areas. I realized the encounter was not just for me personally to get my direction from Higher Authority and to check off missions accomplished as they occurred in the weeks, months, and years following the wreck, all the way to over twenty-seven years after the tragedy. Although I have not seen him again, based upon what has happened, I believe the angel has continued to work behind the scenes for over twenty-seven years up to today. Sharing the story is part of the broader mandate to help others. With its evidence of resurrection and salvation, my encounter must be shared with others. After twenty-seven years of proving itself, there is no doubt about its eternal truth. It shows God's plans to save and sustain us. My encounter and its continuing effects spotlight God's intimate interaction with us as individuals. He is not an aloof deity frowning down on us. He is our own personal God and Savior caring for us infinitely and eternally.

Based upon my experience, I believe that everyone has one or more angels. You may not have seen your angels personally as I saw mine. It may not have been necessary so far for your angels to become visible to you in order to minister to you, protect you, and meet your needs. God's angels are working behind the scenes on your behalf. Be receptive to God's will and consider those thoughts that may suddenly come to mind for your benefit consistent with God's Plans and His Love and concern for you. The angel in my encounter was not just my personal supernatural paramedic. The angel's outstretched hand of healing is for everyone, not just me, and shows God's concern for us as part of His Family. He cares for us as a parent loves a child. He wants us to have life and have it more abundantly.

He holds those accountable who harm us and blesses those who help us. God ultimately overpowers the evil forces attacking us. If He allows us to suffer, it is not in vain. He is there to give us the final victory if we accept Him in faith.

CHAPTER 39
IN GOD WE TRUST

By now it is obvious why we have our national motto, "In God We Trust." This motto is placed on our money to remind us to trust in God and not in our money. With our recession losses, this is an especially timely and pointed reminder. It is God who gets us through recessions, wars, and other challenges both personally and as a nation. Our money is here today and gone tomorrow, but God is there for us for eternity. He provides resources when we have none. He encourages us when we are discouraged or have given up. When our human exertions are exhausted, God intervenes for us, showing His Mighty Hand when all else has failed.

It is not a one-way relationship where we simply rely on God, although ultimately relying upon God rather than ourselves is absolutely essential. While we trust in God, He also wants us to be responsible and participate in His plans for us. We don't get a free ride. God has a bicycle built for two. It is important to realize God is not on our side when he helps us win wars. We are victorious because we are on His side. He strengthens us to be a force for good in the world, a leader who does what is right in His sight. He wants us to be the strongest nation rather than some other country that is bent on evil. If we are not the world's sole superpower, who will take over that role from us? If we are not a responsible world leader with the power God has given us, He can replace us.

At times my encounter with the angel recedes into the past but then is activated again by additional events. My major role in national defense was apparently finished thirteen years ago when I retired from the Navy, but now recent events are reviving some of the same issues that occurred earlier. Rather than exercising good financial management in all areas, defense cuts are being targeted to cut the end-strength numbers of our armed forces. Military procurement is also adversely impacted. Purchases of necessary equipment and weapons systems would be reduced. Worn out airplanes and equipment would not be replaced. Our armed forces would be left short of necessary equipment and resources to fight effectively and win expeditiously with lower casualties and lower costs.

With these recurring issues re-emerging again, I may re-enter the arena of national defense issues as the angel directed me if God again enables and sends me. God is our ultimate Defender. God is in control over our human plans, looking over the efforts of our leaders and ultimately overcoming their and our errors.

jumped by as much as 1,500 riders a day this week.

A Metrorail spokesman credited the heavier ridership to last Sunday's changes in 33 county bus routes designed to coordinate with the schedule of the new mass transit rail system. Those changes, in many cases, left bus riders with

routes which go to the Civic Center area," said Metrorail spokesman Roger Doucha.

On Monday, the first weekday of the new bus routes, Metrorail ridership jumped to 8,663, up from 7,184 a week earlier. Tuesday ridership was 8,886, up from 7,505 the previous week. On Wednesday

"Right at the end of the school year a lot of people take a break and go on vacation," he said. "I think to some degree a lot of people were waiting for school to get out and take their vacations. Now they have done that, and they are back and riding Metrorail.

Woman, child die in car collision

A head-on collision on Biscayne Boulevard has resulted in the death of a woman and her 18-month-old daughter. The father remained hospitalized today in critical condition.

Police said the accident on Biscayne Boulevard and Northeast 105th Street occurred shortly before 10 p.m. yesterday when the family's Toyota was struck by a 1979 Dodge pickup truck. The pickup was traveling north on the boulevard on the wrong side of the

road, said Metro communications Sgt. George Johnson.

The southbound Toyota had just stopped at a traffic light when the truck hit it, Johnson said. The pickup truck overturned in the collision.

Ronalie Elliott Bell, 34, trapped inside the car's wreckage, died at the scene. Her daughter, Ronalie Elizabeth, was pulled from the car and rushed to North Miami General Hospital, where she died.

The father, 41-year-old Robert

Bell, was in critical condition today at North Miami General.

Metro police arrested David McManus, 34, near the scene.

McManus was found wading in a nearby canal in waist-deep water, Johnson said. He was arrested on charges of driving with a suspended license and leaving the scene of an accident where a death occurred. The police charges are preliminary pending a determination by the State Attorney's Office.

ABOUT THE AUTHOR

Coming from a small-town southern family with a rural background, Bob Bell had achieved more than he ever thought possible for an ordinary person who lacked wealth, power, position and prestige. A graduate of Emory University School of Law in Atlanta, GA, he served as a Navy Reserve JAG Commander with eighteen years of service. He also handled civilian claims in thirty-one nations on six continents for iconic insurance companies including Lloyd's of London. His achievements exceeded his wildest dreams when he was growing up. He felt he had reached the highest pinnacle of his career and wanted to spend more time with his family. Then a terrible tragedy and an unexpected, explosive, extended encounter with an angel hurled him back into the arena of life's struggles to engage forces and participate in epic events that were beyond his imagination until his eyes were opened by the angel. The angel instilled the will to continue living and gave Bob his orders from Higher Authority. Bob became fully rededicated and was now a man with overpowering missions from above that he could never forget or abandon. If he messed up, he would not only hurt himself but also many others while disastrously failing to follow God's will.

After being re-directed by the angel, Bob served an additional fourteen years with the Navy, reaching thirty-two years of combined Federal Service on active duty, in the reserves and as a civilian employee. During his extended years of service after his encounter with the angel, from 1993-1995 Bob was National President of the Naval Reserve Association with over 20,000 officers as members (now the Association of the United States Navy). He received medals and numerous commendations including three Armed Forces Reserve Medals and Certificates of Appreciation from President Bill Clinton and the head of the Navy Reserve Law Program. Bob served during the terms of seven Presidents from Lyndon Johnson to Bill Clinton, but his last fourteen years of service and all of his successful national defense work during that time resulted from his encounter with the angel.

CONVERSATION GUIDE

Frequently Asked Questions and Answers

Chapters 1 and 3

1. What actions of the angel authenticated that he came from God?

(a) He arrived in a spectacular supernatural manner.

(b) He came in answer to Muffin's urgent plea (prayer) to God.

(c) He came to help, pushing the pickup truck away from Bob.

(d) He was taking Muffin and Elizabeth to Heaven.

(e) He showed compassion to Bob, helping Bob understand his life was not over.

(f) He wanted to make sure the driver of the pickup truck was punished. [Compare NIV, Romans, 13:3-4, "He [the ruler] does not bear the sword for nothing. He is God's servant, an agent of wrath to bring punishment to the wrongdoer."

(g) He also spoke to Bob about facing judgment and the need to be right with God.

(h) He used supernatural power to heal Bob's broken bones.

(i) He could see into the future as only God can. [Compare NIV, Isaiah, 46:10, "I make known the end from the beginning, from ancient times, what is still to come...."]

(j) He had authority to assign missions in life to Bob. These missions were the type of work that is consistent with God's character. [Compare NIV, Ephesians, 2:10, "For we are God's workmanship, created in Christ Jesus to do good works, which God prepared in advance for us to do."]

(k) He had power and authority to send Bob back from the dead to life. [Compare NIV, Luke, 20:36, "and they can no longer die; for they are like the angels. They are God's children, since they are children of the resurrection." Also, Luke 20:38, "He is not the God of the dead, but of the living, for to him all are alive." Compare NIV, John, 11:25, "Jesus said to her, "I am the resurrection and the life. He who believes in me will live, even though he dies; and whoever lives and believes in me will never die."...."]

(l) The information he provided about the future all proved true over time.

2.   Why did Bob not cry out to God when Muffin did?

(a) Bob was still trying to control a situation that was out of control.

(b) He was watching the answer to Muffin's plea as the angel appeared.

(c) He was trying to turn the car some so the impact would be on his side, hoping to save Muffin and Elizabeth.

Chapter 2

1.   Do you think God sent the "Good Samaritan" lady who stopped at the wreck?

2.   What clues point to her possible heavenly connection?

3.   What do you think of her appearing again later and then disappearing without a trace?

4.   Do you think she was a guardian angel?

5.   When she appeared later at the hospital, why do you think she wanted to make sure Bob was OK?

6.   Why did the young teenage bystander at the wreck pursue the pickup truck driver and then turn him in to the police?

(a) The wreck was so bad he felt compelled to help.

(b) He felt the driver of the pickup truck had committed a serious crime and was trying to get away.

Chapter 4

1. When Bob returned to life, why did he struggle to move?

(a) The paramedics had found he was dead and were ready to take him to the morgue.

2. Why did Bob tell the doctors at the hospital that he was one of their lawyers?

(a) They were not going to treat him because he was a lawyer.

(b) He had to show the doctors he was on their side and not a risk to them.

(c) He truthfully referred to some of his past legal work to obtain treatment.

3. When the doctors decided to treat Bob, what was done first?

(a) Two complete sets of X-rays were taken showing no broken bones as reported by the paramedics at the wreck.

(b) Realizing now that Bob could survive, the doctors hurried to treat him extensively and placed him in intensive care.

4. How did the plastic surgeon obtain photographs of Bob to use in repairing Bob's face? Why did the plastic surgeon decide not to remove smaller embedded glass fragments from Bob's forehead and scalp?

(a) Bob's cousin John drove across the city in the middle of the night to the hospital bringing family photographs and consented to Bob's treatments as next of kin.

(b) The plastic surgeon said using a surgical knife to remove smaller embedded glass fragments would do more harm than good, so he left them embedded in Bob's flesh.

5. How do you explain the difference between the hospital X-rays showing no broken bones and the paramedics' report from the wreck that every bone in Bob's body was broken?

(a) The angel healed him after the paramedics' findings before the X-rays were taken.

(b) The paramedics were completely incorrect?

Chapters 5, 7, and 8

1. How and when did Bob grieve the losses of Muffin and Elizabeth?

(a) After the initial shock of their losses, at the end of each day in the hospital when Bob was alone trying to go to sleep in his hospital bed, he experienced flashbacks to their lives together.

(b) While grieving through these flashbacks, it was both very painful and also comforting to some extent. It was a way to cling to them through these memories.

(c) Bob again focused on grieving at the evening wake for Muffin and Elizabeth. This was very painful, but he received some relief from his anguish at the memorial service the next day because there was so much praise for the positive lives of Muffin and Elizabeth; and there was reassurance resulting from his encounter with the angel and what was seen then. Bob realized he was blessed to have Muffin and Elizabeth, making their losses even more painful and doubly devastating for him. Because of his exceptionally strong bond with Muffin and Elizabeth, he excruciatingly felt the ferocious losses he was suffering.

Chapters 6 and 9

1. Why was Bob moved from the ICU to a private room in the hospital?

(a) Although he was paralyzed from the waist down and predicted to never walk again, his condition had stabilized.

(b) He could have visitors who wanted to see him to try to comfort him.

2. Why did Uncle Bill ask if Bob needed anything, and what was Bob's request?

(a) Uncle Bill wanted to help, and he was the relative who lived closest to the hospital. He felt he could quickly go to his house and return to the hospital to help Bob.

(b) Bob asked for a large salad. That was the only food he craved, and he was hungry.

3. Why did Bob rudely eat the entire salad in front of his visitors when it was planned to be enough salad for several days (and he ate it right out of the large serving bowl in which Uncle Bill brought the salad)?

(a) Bob had not had any real food in several days. He was very hungry.

(b) He liked salads. It was one of his favorite foods.

(c) Hospital food was depressing, but the salad was a really good, healthy salad that boosted Bob's spirits.

(d) Bob felt his visitors would understand. They were encouraging him to eat the salad and curious to see how much he could eat.

4. Why did the plastic surgeon stop at Bob's room, and what did he want to do after he examined Bob?

(a) He was making some rounds at the hospital and thought Bob might not come to his office later for follow up after leaving the hospital.

(b) He wanted to drill a small hole in Bob's head to help relieve the pressure from Bob's severe concussion.

5. What was the result of the plastic surgeon's drilling into Bob's head?

(a) When the drill broke through the bone, Bob paralysis was instantly relieved.

(b) Bob and his visitors celebrated, and Bob thought this was part of the angel's promise that he would be healed. He was encouraged that there would be more progress toward a full recovery.

6. Why did the "Good Samaritan" from the wreck reappear at Bob's hospital room and then disappear without a trace?

7. Do you think she was really another guardian angel?

8. What do you think about the beach towel with the unusual geometric pattern that she left behind? Do you think the beach towel was used as a celestial marker to pinpoint the location of Bob's body so the life-restoring and healing energy from the angel could be aimed there?

9. Why was Bob in a big hurry to progress with physical therapy and willing to push against the pain barrier until he could barely endure the effort to move more?

(a) His muscles would deteriorate permanently if not used normally again soon.

(b) He needed to get back on his feet so he could work again. He had no other income.

(c) He was alone with no one to take care of him. He must be able to care for himself.

10. Why did Bob want to hire a lawyer while he was in the hospital?

(a) He was thinking of the angel saying to bring the pickup truck driver to justice.

(b) Delay in working on the case would make it more difficult to obtain evidence.

(c) Although Bob was brought back to life, his broken bones were healed and his paralysis from the waist down was relieved as the angel said, bringing the pickup truck driver to justice was the first mission the angel stated in the encounter.

(d) Bringing the pickup truck driver to justice should be Bob's top priority. It was brought up first by the angel and was an immediate, urgent concern. Some of the other missions could come later, possibly much later.

11. Why did Bob call Steve Tarr to help him?

(a) Bob wanted to comply with Muffin's desire to help Steve's son obtain funding for graduate work at Emory University.

(b) Bob was hospitalized and disabled. He could not act quickly as needed.

12. Why did Steve Tarr initially refuse to come to the hospital to help Bob?

(a) Steve Tarr was a very ethical lawyer and did not want to "chase ambulances."

(b) After Bob explained the urgency, Steve agreed to help, and he came to the hospital with his investigator to take photographs of Bob's injuries and to interview Bob.

(c) Although Steve and his investigator got to work right away, Steve would not let Bob sign a fee contract until Bob was out of the hospital and not taking pain medication.

13. Why did Bob start working with his office by telephone from his hospital bed?

(a) Bob's largest claim needed immediate attention.

(b) Bob wanted to show his clients that he was able to take care of business.

Chapters 10, 11, and 12

1. When did Bob realize the doctors left him with no pain killing medication?

(a) It was after he was discharged from the hospital when he was at the Elliotts' home.

(b) It was when it was time to take his medication again and after it was too late to obtain a prescription from the hospital doctors.

2. How did Bob progress with his therapy and recovery?

(a) He was initially in and out of the Elliotts' swimming pool from his wheelchair.

(b) Then he went home where there were several split levels, and he switched from his wheelchair to a walker to get past the level changes.

(c) He gradually increased the time he was working each day, and he started driving again before he could walk because he needed to shop for necessary supplies.

(d) When he began walking haltingly, he would go to court early and leave late so no one would notice his handicap and target him as vulnerable or disabled. He did the same thing at Navy receptions, placing himself in the middle of expected activity before anyone arrived and leaving late, again to avoid being noticed negatively.

3. After Steve Tarr was officially representing Bob's claims from the wreck, what book of the Bible did Steve recommend for Bob to read and why?

(a) The Book of Job because it helps show how to cope with suffering.

4. When Bob was turned back on his way to the cemetery by a Voice asking, "Why seek ye the living among the dead?", where is this question also found in the Bible?

(a) In KJV, Luke 24:5, the angels spoke these same words to Mary Magdalene, Johanna, Mary the mother of James and others who came to the empty tomb looking for the body of Jesus that was not there.

5. Why did Bob perform his FY 1984 active duty toward the end of September and his FY 1985 active duty in early October at the beginning of the next Fiscal Year?

(a) He wanted to make sure he had a satisfactory year completed for FY 1984.

(b) He wanted to make a strong start in FY 1985 and have 2 successful periods of active duty before anyone could question his physical fitness to perform duty.

(c) He wanted to be completely up to date in performance of duty before his next regular physical/medical examination in early 1985 [February].

Chapters 13 and 14

1. Why was Bob discouraged about the lack of progress in the criminal case?

(a) Helping bring the driver of the pickup truck to justice was Bob's first major mission from the angel when Bob was sent back to life.

(b) Although the angel was right about so many facts including the amount of Bob's car insurance and locating an eyewitness to the wreck overlooked by the police, no prior criminal records could be found other than one minor prior traffic stop in Florida.

(c) Although the angel must be right, the lack of significant prior criminal records was very perplexing and could result in the pickup truck driver as a first offender not being punished, even if he was found guilty after pleading not guilty.

(d) Bob was tormented by the prospect of failure in the criminal case.

2. In early December, 1984, how did Bob's first necessary business trip to New York after the wreck provide some encouragement concerning the criminal case?

(a) His Navy friends in New York hosted him for lunch at the Europa Café and promised to investigate the nearby Connecticut and New York past of the pickup truck driver.

(b) Bob appreciated this friendly gesture. He did not know if anything could be found, but he felt better that someone else would be looking in addition to the police personnel in Miami who had found nothing. Bob trusted the angel and his New York friends. They were lawyers!

Chapters 15, 16, and 17

1. How did Bob get through the first Christmas and New Year's without Muffin and Elizabeth?

(a) He went to Europe for over two weeks, spending most of the time with Muffin's sister and her husband who was a doctor in a small village in Austria.

(b) This big break was not a pure escape for Bob from his troubles because he had to work in Milan, Italy on January 2, 1985. However, his work schedule enabled him to spend two weeks with relatives in Austria until January 1, 1985.

2. On his flight from Frankfurt, Germany to Linz, Austria, what caused Bob to suddenly focus on national defense issues as the angel had shown him?

(a) From the airplane window he saw Soviet tanks massed in an attack formation along the border between Austria and Czechoslovakia.

(b) While in Austria, he obtained more information about the Soviet threat.

3. When Bob arrived very late at night in frozen Linz, how was he like an ant trying to move something much bigger than himself?

(a) He had so much luggage and no help to move it right down the main street from the bus station to the train station.

(b) He moved one piece of luggage at a time until he had moved the entire pile some.

4. While Bob was resting in the village as a guest of his relatives, how did he begin to respond to the national defense mission he received from the angel?

(a) He read a book about the U.S. Embassy hostage crisis in Iran.

(b) He studied Middle Eastern and terrorism issues and reviewed his prior projects for the Navy that could help in the future.

5. How did Bob get the "worst blizzard in forty years in Europe" as a "birthday present"?

(a) The weather took a turn for the worst as his 42nd birthday approached, and the Danube River froze over at Vienna which it usually did not do.

(b) The weather was so severe it immobilized everybody and everything. Even with his warmest clothes, Bob from Miami was affected more than his relatives and others.

6. How was Christmas in Austria with Bob's relatives different from Christmas at home in America?

(a) There was much less emphasis on giving and receiving gifts. The family celebration of Christmas on Christmas Eve was more like a family reunion.

(b) There was a live Christmas tree with lighted candles instead of electric lights.

(c) The Christmas family reunions continued after Christmas with other relatives including a lunch stop in a nearby town en route to Vienna.

7. How was catsup a gesture of international goodwill?

(a) Bob's Austrian lunch hosts offered catsup to him because he is American.

(b) Bob declined the catsup because their food was so good without any catsup.

8. How did the national defense issue come up again during the family lunch stop?

(a) Some of the relatives who were electrical engineers talked about the power sharing grid between the Soviet Bloc and Western Europe that could be used militarily.

(b) The Austrians wanted their neutrality to be protected from Soviet intervention.

9. How did Bob get a history lesson in Vienna with the family?

(a) Christian explained everything we saw during our visit from World War I up to date.

(b) We visited one of the old royal palaces that is a museum, and the guide was very good explaining everything.

10. How did Bob depart Vienna on January 1, 1985 to travel to Milan?

(a) Very early in the morning walking across the main plaza through ice, snow, and broken glass from the New Year's celebration to meet a taxi he booked.

(b) At the airport he was forced into first class, violating his usual international travel safety procedures to keep a low profile as an American abroad, and then, over the Alps, there was a false alarm about hijacking the airplane.

(c) Bob was relieved to finally arrive in Milan, but there were new threats there.

11. What happened in Milan?

(a) The hotel staff asked Bob to keep the heavy metal shutters closed over the windows for protection against terrorist [Red Brigade] attacks.

(b) Bob met with his client's representative, and they obtained the witness statements.

(c) They finished work early and went shopping for gifts to bring home.

(d) The shopping was very successful but involved comical circumstances.

(e) As Bob was departing Milan, the bomb sniffing dogs came through the airport.

Chapter 18

1. When Bob returned home, what was the situation there?

(a) There was no progress with the criminal case.

(b) The search for prior criminal records continued to be futile.

(c) Bob was depressed and wondering how the angel could be right about everything else, but not this, the first and most important reason for Bob to continue living.

2. What caused Bob to be sorry that he doubted the angel?

(a) Late in the afternoon before the court hearing early the next morning, Bob received a telephone call from one of his New York friends with good news.

(b) The pickup truck driver's prior criminal records in Connecticut and New York had been located and were being sent overnight to Miami.

(c) The defendant changed his plea to guilty and was sentenced at a separate hearing.

(d) This part of Bob's life involving the aftermath of the wreck was now over, but questions remained about the future and how the other missions from the angel would develop.

Chapters 19, 20, and 21

1. After the criminal case was closed, how did Bob make a concerted effort during the first half of 1985 to pursue the path to recovery?

(a) He passed his Navy physical in February, 1985.

(b) He got a second opinion from a respected orthopedic doctor.

(c) He began a regular strenuous exercise program.

(d) He spent more time in warm showers so glass fragments could come out of his skin.

(e) He completed his sessions with the psychiatrist hired by the insurance company.

(f) He focused more on work.

(g) He planned a business trip to London to strengthen his position there.

2. How did the national defense issue suddenly come up as Bob was working toward a personal comeback and preparing to depart for London?

(a) Bob received a telephone call from a Navy captain at Navy Headquarters in Norfolk with a new, important assignment.

(b) He carefully considered this call because the captain said he called so Bob would not be surprised later, and the angel said Bob would not be surprised, that he would know what to do when the time comes.

(c) Bob considered the significance of the timing of the call and decided to look for helpful information in London. He also thought about his previous experience that could help with this new, important assignment.

3. While in London, how did Bob find a key reference for his new Navy assignment?

(a) He decided to look in law bookstores he knew about in London because his assignment was for the legal portion of the Navy project.

(b) He stumbled into a different type of bookstore and found a newly issued book hidden on the bottom shelf in a corner. This book was exactly what was needed and was not available anywhere else or any other way at that time.

4.   What else did Bob do while he was in London?

(a) He enjoyed the historical celebration of the 40th Anniversary of Victory in Europe.

(b) He attended a maritime industry/insurance dinner.

(c) He met with clients and worked on their claims.

(d) He met with Jeremy Thomas and visited with Jeremy and his family.

(e) Bob saw his own relatives at Westminster Abbey and learned more history there.

Chapters 22 and 23

1.   How was Bob's personal comeback campaign interrupted by more bad news?

(a) After returning from London and attending the Navy project staff meeting in Norfolk on May 18, his mother was being re-admitted to the hospital on May 20 for cancer that recurred after an earlier surgery.

(b) His mother's condition had worsened, and her outlook was bleak.

(c) At the same time, Bob learned that he had been passed over for promotion to captain. He was ready to give up and wondered again if the angel finally missed something.

2.   Although she was very sick, she was still Mom, and she really got after Bob to try again!

(a) To satisfy his mother at first, Bob did what she said.

(b) As Bob was making a second effort, there were encouraging developments along the way, and he renewed and increased his efforts to be promoted.

(c) He continued with the Navy project in Norfolk and was elected National Vice President for Legal Affairs of the Navy Reserve Association at its national meeting in Norfolk in early October, but his mother was dying; and she passed away while he was returning from Norfolk. She expressed her strong faith in the resurrection in Bob's last visit with her before he went to Norfolk.

3.   After returning from his mother's funeral, what series of good news items developed?

(a) Bob received very good fitness reports from the Military Justice Division Captain in Washington for his active duty work and for commanding his reserve unit there.

(b) Bob was notified he would receive a letter of commendation from the Navy commodore commanding the Key West/Straits of Florida exercise project that Bob worked on in London and at Norfolk from May to August, 1985.

(c) Bob was able to go to London for the Christmas holidays and then return home for some quiet time before the holidays and 1985 ended.

(d) In 1986, Bob received orders for another exercise in Norfolk and received an excellent fitness report from an Air Force general. This fitness report was delivered to the Selection Board in Washington, and Bob was promoted to captain.

(e) He learned his record was complete when it was considered by the Selection Board, and he had worked for most members of the Selection Board.

(f) After learning about his promotion, Bob made an enjoyable, eventful trip to Vancouver, British Columbia in June, 1986 combining business, pleasure, national defense insight, and Expo 86. He was comically mistaken for the Governor of British Columbia and met some special friends there.

(g) As a result of his earlier successful work in Norfolk, he was asked to work at Navy Headquarters there in November, 1986 and again in October, 1987.

4. How did Bob see proof the angel showed him the actual future as it was happening?

(a) Two years after the wreck he saw a defense video showing exactly the same events.

(b) Bob verified that the video was taken ten months after the wreck. The events were still in the future when the wreck occurred. It had not happened yet at that time.

5. How did the angel help Bob focus on areas of national defense where Bob should help?

(a) Three years after the wreck, Bob was attending a national meeting of the Navy Reserve Association in Phoenix, Arizona. The admiral who was the head of the Navy Reserve was outlining national defense needs, especially those of the Navy.

(b) As the admiral continued to speak, he looked more and more like the angel. The admiral's resemblance to the angel became so overpowering that Bob had to look away until the admiral finished speaking.

(c) Bob realized the angel was telling him to listen carefully to the admiral and to help with these national defense needs, especially those involving the Navy.

Chapters 24, 25, and 26

1. As more time passed, how and when did Bob focus on other more personal areas of the vision the angel showed him during the encounter?

(a) Around two years after the wreck, Bob thought more and more about the girl the angel showed him in a vision and decided he should try to find her.

(b) For almost two more years, Bob looked for her, but he failed to find her.

(c) Bob finally realized he could not find her until God revealed her again.

2. When and from whom did Bob receive unexpected help in finding the girl?

(a) Rosalie Elliott telephoned with information about a girl Bob should meet.

(b) Bob met Raymie at a church singles' luau by a small lake at the home of a friend of Rosalie Elliott who was also a friend of Raymie.

(c) Bob followed up with Raymie. She could be the girl in the vision. She seemed to fit.

(d) Bob wanted confirmation Raymie was the girl in the vision.

3. How did Bob realize Raymie was really the girl in the vision?

(a) More and more similarities became apparent, but Bob was not sure because in the vision he only saw a side view of the girl.

(b) Returning in the late afternoon from an outing to Everglades National Park, Raymie had her hair pulled back, and she fell asleep in the front passenger seat as Bob was driving. The last rays of direct sunlight at sunset shone on the left side of Raymie's face and then faded out so she looked exactly like the girl in the vision.

(c) Bob suddenly realized in a split second the girl in the vision was asleep beside him; he was so amazed he momentarily drove off the edge of the road's pavement.

(d) When Bob told Raymie about the encounter, she did not think he was crazy.

4. How did Raymie and Bob move toward marriage in six months?

(a) Everything was perfect; they were in agreement; and they were in love!

(b) They gratefully realized their meeting was orchestrated by God through others.

(c) Raymie planned details of the wedding while Bob requested a military wedding.

5. What were some of the special moments of the military part of the wedding?

(a) Bob and the other officers were in Service Dress White uniforms.

(b) There was a spectacular arch of swords just outside the front of the church as Raymie and Bob left the church at the end of the wedding.

(c) At the reception, Raymie and Bob cut their wedding cake with Bob's Navy sword.

6. Where did Raymie and Bob go for their honeymoon, and how was it kept secret?

(a) They went into seclusion at a small hotel at the nearby Grove Isle Club?

(b) The car was valet parked there ahead of time, and Bob took a taxi back to the church. Then Raymie and Bob took a limousine from the reception to the Grand Bay Hotel for dinner and then after dinner to the Grove Isle Club hotel.

Chapter 27

1. After their wedding and honeymoon in October, 1988, what trips followed for Raymie and Bob in November and December, 1988?

(a) There was a trip with English friends across the Everglades to Marco Island, Florida for the national meeting of The Maritime Law Association of the United States.

(b) There was another trip to Washington for Bob to work at the Pentagon.

(c) In December, Raymie and Bob went to Baton Rouge for Christmas, receiving the horrible news en route about the tragic bombing of the Pan Am flight from London.

(d) There was nothing they could do, so they resolved to enjoy their first Christmas.

2. Why was Bob working at the Pentagon, and how did this relate to the encounter?

(a) After four times working at Navy Headquarters in Norfolk, his boss there told him it was time for Bob to go work at The Pentagon.

(b) Bob's first duty there prepared him for future work at a higher level of national defense and involved him in major terrorism issues as foretold by the angel.

Chapters 28 and 29

1. How did Bob's rising role in national defense bring him to higher levels of involvement?

(a) He continued to work at The Pentagon, and following the victory in Desert Storm, he was elected later in 1991 as National Executive Vice President of the Navy Reserve Association, next in line for the top position.

(b) Having already served two years as National Vice President for Legislation, Bob fought against deep defense cuts in 1992 as the angel charged him in the encounter.

2. How were Bob's efforts involving military preparedness suddenly interrupted, and how did he try to serve some other way?

(a) Following Hurricane Andrew, he was suddenly dumped as National Executive Vice President at a national meeting in Arizona, raising doubts about the angel's agenda.

(b) He sought statewide elected office in Florida, but his campaigning brought him more involvement in national defense rather than political success.

3. How was Raymie's health protected as promised by the angel?

(a) She survived emergency surgery after Emily's birth in 1989.

(b) She survived pneumonia in February, 1993 after the church prayer chain was activated.

4. How was Bob restored to a leadership role in national defense?

(a) The people he met campaigning encouraged him, and he heard there was discontent with the officer who replaced him in the Navy Reserve Association office.

(b) After an uphill battle, Bob was elected National President of the Navy Reserve Association in October, 1993 in the hometown of his principal opponent.

Chapter 30

1. What was Bob's new mission toward the end of 1993, and how was it consistent with the agenda of the angel in the encounter?

(a) Raymie and Bob adopted a daughter from an orphanage in Odessa, Ukraine.

(b) This was part of the mission from the angel to help others, but it was much more personal within their family.

(c) Caitlyn needed an open-heart surgery as soon as possible. If Bob had not survived the wreck, this may not have occurred.

Chapters 31, 32, 33, 34, and 35

1. When Bob was national president of the Navy Reserve Association from October, 1993 to September, 1995, what were three major national defense accomplishments that may not have occurred if he had not survived the wreck in 1984? Can you discuss details?

(a) Building the "10thth" nuclear-powered aircraft carrier, the USS George Washington.

(b) Passage of a catch up pay increase for all military personnel.

(c) Authorization for a third huge hunter-killer Sea Wolf submarine.

2. After Bob performed his last duty at The Pentagon in August, 1995, and after he completed his two years as national president of the Navy Reserve Association in September, 1995, what did he do for the next three years?

(a) He worked at the U.S. Southern Command Headquarters in Miami through June, 1998 as a reserve officer in the legal office.

(b) He assisted with a military conference in Miami attended by high ranking officers from almost all western hemisphere nations.

(c) He worked on the issue of military cooperation with Mexico.

(d) He retired from the Navy July 1, 1998 and had a retirement ceremony aboard the USS Cole at Port Everglades, Florida in October, 1998.

3. What did Bob do after he was fully retired from the Navy?

(a) He made plans to move to Baton Rouge to be close to Raymie's family.

(b) He helped his church in Coral Gables, Florida find a pastor.

(c) A home in Baton Rouge was purchased, and the house in Florida was sold.

(d) He finished his last case in Florida at Key West in October, 2000.

(e) The children were placed in Christian schools in Baton Rouge.

(f) Emily had surgery for appendicitis in September, 2000, and Bob recovered from pneumonia in July and August, 2001.

4. In September, 2001 the weather in Baton Rouge was beautiful and the transition was going more smoothly after the house in Florida was finally sold in June, 2001, but what happened that turned Bob's attention back to national defense; and how did he react?

(a) America was under surprise attack on September 11.

(b) The terrorist attacks clarified the angel's agenda including the significance through seventeen intervening years of Bob's missions from the encounter in 1984.

(c) Bob more fully realized that his assignments from the angel were not just a "laundry list" of things that needed to be done but that history could have developed differently if he had not survived the wreck in 1984 and these missions had remained undone.

(d) He was asked to be a resource for a local television station, explaining terrorism, the Navy's role in the war (including "his" aircraft carrier the George Washington) and important aspects of international law.

(e) He became more involved in helping others and taught world history and western civilization, sharing some of his experiences.

Chapters 36 and 37

1. How did helping others suddenly involve a new dimension on a much larger scale?

(a) Hurricanes Katrina, Rita, and Wilma struck in 2005, flooding parts of New Orleans and other areas.

(b) Bob became involved in the largest ever missing persons search, locating survivors and identifying casualties.

(c) For almost nine months, he had a key role in locating thousands of missing persons and documenting their current addresses.

(d) When the mission was substantially accomplished, the remaining cases were returned to local authorities for resolution.

(e) Bob then went to work with a Fortune 500 company that was involved in a major response to the hurricane losses, helping them manage collections and cash flow.

Chapters 38 and 39

1. Do you think sharing his story is Bob's last major mission from the encounter with the angel? If not, what other missions from the angel's agenda might be ongoing?

2. Do you believe Bob's entire story? If you believe all of it or none of it, what are your reasons? If you believe part of it, what parts do you believe, and why?

3. If you don't believe the entire story, what parts do you not believe and why.

4. What parts of the book did you enjoy, and what parts did you not like? Why?

5. Where in the book would you like more details and more explanations?

6. Are you surprised that our national defense was part of the angel's agenda?

7. Do you think Bob's mission concerning national defense was completed when he retired from the Navy in 1998? If not, why not? If you think it was completed, why?

8. Do you think Bob should become involved again in national defense issues? What is the basis of your opinion?

9. Do you think he will become involved again? Why?

10. Why do you think Bob believes that we trust in God for our national defense and in our other areas of concern?

11. Would you like to meet Capt. Bob Bell and hear him speak about the book's events? You can contact him through the website at www.encounterpublishingllc.com.

Made in United States
North Haven, CT
04 April 2024

50914660R00134